EARLY CHILDHOOD EDUCATION/
PRESCHOOL TEACHER
CAREER STARTER

EARLY CHILDHOOD EDUCATION/
PRESCHOOL TEACHER
career starter

**Elizabeth Chesla
and Jelena Matic**

WITHDRAWN

LEARNINGEXPRESS

New York

Library of Congress Cataloging-in-Publication Data:
Chesla, Elizabeth L.
    Early childhood education/preschool teacher career starter / Elizabeth
Chesla and Jelena Matic.—1st ed.
        p. cm.
Includes bibliographical references.
    ISBN 1-57685-409-4
    1. Early childhood education—Vocational guidance—United States.
2. Preschool teaching—Vocational guidance—United States. 3. Early
childhood teachers—United States. I. Matic, Jelena. II. Title.
    LB1775.6 .C54 2002
    372.21'023—dc21

                                                    2002001272

Printed in the United States of America
9 8 7 6 5 4 3 2 1
First Edition

ISBN 1-57685-409-4

For more information or to place an order, contact LearningExpress at:
    900 Broadway
    Suite 604
    New York, NY 10003

Or visit us at:
    www.learnatest.com

About the Authors

Elizabeth Chesla, MA, is Director of the Technical and Professional Communications Program at New York City's Polytechnic University. She is the author of several books, including *Read Better, Remember More; Write Better Essays in Just 20 Minutes a Day;* and *A Parent's Guide to 8th Grade.* She lives in West Orange, New Jersey with her husband and son.

Jelena Matic is a doctoral student of chemical engineering at New York City's Polytechnic University. She has worked as a teaching assistant, adjunct instructor, and has written for McGraw-Hill's magazine, *Chemical Engineering.* She loves taking care of children.

Contents

Contents

Acknowledgments

OUR GRATITUDE to all the early childhood educators who shared their stories and expertise to help make this book possible. We extend a special thanks to Dr. Deborah Ceglowski, Amy Flynn, Megan Friday, Krista Harper, and Amy Quigley for their input and guidance.

Introduction

Why Enter the Field of Early Childhood Education?

YOU HAVE picked up this book because you are interested in early childhood education—one of the most rewarding careers you can choose, and a field in which job opportunities have never been better.

This book will give you a good sense of what being an early childhood educator is all about. You will learn what early childhood educators do, why it is such a rewarding career, and whether or not it is the right job for you. You will also find out about different positions in the early childhood education field, how to find the degree and certificate program that is right for you, how to apply for financial aid, how to find a job, and how to succeed once you have landed a job.

As you read through this book, you will see that early childhood education is a career with numerous and diverse opportunities. From being a part-time teacher's aide to the director of a large day care, from being a nanny to a preschool teacher, you have many choices. You can work with infants and toddlers, bilingual children, or children with special needs; you can work in a Montessori school, a religiously affiliated institution, an elementary school, or your own home; you can work part time or full time, mornings or afternoons, during the academic year or the whole year through. And you will have many opportunities for professional development and career enhancement along the way.

It is an exciting time for early childhood education, a field that is experiencing healthy job growth as both parents and politicians increasingly recognize its tremendous importance. Research from around the world continues to demonstrate the benefits of early childhood education and provide childcare workers and preschool teachers with a deeper understanding of what they already know to be true: that the early childhood years are critical in a child's social, emotional, intellectual, and physical development. It is a time when many professional organizations and research institutions are working to improve the early childhood profession, and striving to help early childhood educators get the kind of working conditions, pay, and respect they deserve. In addition, more parents are enrolling their children in daycare and preschool and more states are expanding their early childhood education programs, so you will have more job opportunities than ever before should you decide to enter this rewarding field.

Becoming an early childhood educator is an exciting process. Use this book as your guide to the information you need to make the right decisions as you plan your career path. The following table briefly describes each chapter for easy reference so that you see how this book will help plan your career path as an early childhood educator.

Chapter	*Description*
One Hot Jobs: Rewarding Careers in Early Childhood Education	This chapter gives you an overview of early childhood education, including the types of early childhood education jobs and the rich rewards of working with young children. You will learn what it takes to be an early childhood educator, the differences among various early childhood education settings, and what sort of salaries you can expect when you land a job.
Two All About Early Childhood Education Programs	In this chapter, you will get an in-depth view of the variety of programs in early childhood education, the kinds of requirements that you must meet to be accepted into your program, the requirements you must complete, and tips on how to choose the program that is best for you.
Three Financial Aid for the Training and Certification You Need	This chapter describes the process of applying for financial aid, estimating the cost of your education, and guidelines for understanding the federal financial aid formulas, and filling out the FAFSA. It also gives you suggestions on how to find scholarships, grants, loans, and work-study programs.
Four Landing Your First Job: Where and How to Find the Right Position	Now that you know all about programs and financial aid opportunities, this chapter will help you launch your job search. It shows you how to use the Internet, your school, job fairs, and publications and how to network to find out about available positions.

EARLY CHILDHOOD EDUCATION/ PRESCHOOL TEACHER CAREER STARTER

CHAPTER one

HOT JOBS: REWARDING CAREERS IN EARLY CHILDHOOD EDUCATION

FROM ASSISTANT teachers to daycare directors, from nannies to preschool teachers and homecare providers, early childhood educators play a vital role in the nurturing and education of millions of young children across the country. This chapter describes the rich rewards of a career in early childhood education and what it takes to be an effective early childhood educator. You will also learn about the various positions early childhood educators can hold, the kinds of settings in which early childhood educators work, and several areas of specialization within early childhood education. This chapter also provides you with important information about salaries and hiring trends for early childhood educators.

MAYBE YOU HAVE been babysitting ever since you can remember. Maybe you are the oldest child and have spent much of your life helping your parents raise and nurture your siblings. Maybe you have always been fascinated by the amazing speed with which young children learn and develop new skills. Or, maybe you just love being around children, fulfilled by their genuineness and affection and the endless rewards of sharing their company. In any case, you understand the importance of building a strong foundation in the formative early childhood years, and you want to help guide children through this exciting time, supporting and stimulating their social, emotional, intellectual, and physical development. In short, you would like to become an early childhood educator, someone who will have a tremendous impact on the lives of many children.

WHY EARLY CHILDHOOD EDUCATION?
A CAREER WITH MANY REWARDS

Few careers offer the emotional rewards of a career in early childhood education. Despite the typically low salaries and long hours, year after year, hundreds of thousands of early childhood educators find themselves continually fulfilled by their daily interactions with children. Jennifer Simpson, for example, a preschool teacher in Nashville, Tennessee reports, "I like going to work and getting hugs—not many jobs offer that bonus! I also like the many different aspects of the job: I get to plan lessons and implement them, I get to work with children and their parents, and I have a lot of freedom in curriculum planning and activities. I also enjoy watching children soak up every little thing we teach them, especially those children who have not had a supportive educational environment at home. We get to give them experiences and introduce them to ideas they've never been exposed to before. I think that's the best part of this job: enriching children's lives."

Megan Friday, who teaches three to five year olds at Friends' School in Boulder, Colorado, agrees: "I've always loved working with young children. Their growth is so visible and you can see the results of your teaching so quickly. Young children are so eager to learn, to take on greater and greater challenges, and I love being the one to give them the experiences that help them grow. I also love that every day is a new day, a clean slate, because the children live so much in the present. It makes it exciting to go to work."

"Working with kids has made me realize how much love I am capable of giving," adds Irma Mihalovitch, a nanny in Brooklyn, NY. "I enjoy every day I'm with Lukas. I was there when he took one of his first steps, said his first words, made his first friends. It has been immensely rewarding."

Beyond the deep satisfaction that comes from nurturing children and guiding them through the critical formative years, working in early childhood education offers other important rewards. One is the knowledge that your actions will have a long-term impact on the children in your care. When you teach a toddler how to spell his name or button his own coat, for example, you are not just teaching him a practical skill—you are also helping him gain the confidence and independence he needs to develop a strong sense of self-worth and a lifelong love of learning.

Another benefit of a career in early childhood education is that it never gets dull. While you teach, you will always be learning, developing new strategies and skills as you deal with unique children in unique situations. No two children or classrooms will be alike, and you can count on a rich variety of experiences throughout each year as the children in your care learn and grow. "The more I teach, the more I get to keep building on my knowledge of child development," says Friday. "Every year, the children teach me, the parents teach me, and I learn a lot from my colleagues. I get to learn all the time."

Early childhood education is also a career that offers great flexibility. You can work part or full time, caring for children for two hours, three mornings each week or eight hours a day, five days a week. You can teach art to four-year-olds in an after-school program or tend to the needs of a group of infants in an extended-day childcare center. You can specialize in bilingual education or work with children with special needs, with at-risk children in an inner city school, or with gifted children in an enriched school readiness program. In addition, you can always take advantage of continuing education and other professional development activities to advance your career or move into a particular area of specialization.

That is what Gabby Norris of Tampa, Florida, did. "I always knew I wanted to work with young children," says Norris, "but until I started looking into early childhood education I didn't realize how many options I had. I started as a nanny right after high school and took some early childhood education courses at night to get a degree. After I took a course called Working with Exceptional Children, I realized I wanted to focus on special education. Now I work in a preschool where most of the children have developmental delays or mild retardation. Some days are difficult, of course, but I love the challenge, and I can't imagine any career being more rewarding."

Friday also finds professional development an important part of what she enjoys about her job. "In the past five years, I've really expanded my knowledge base by attending early childhood education conferences. It's really rewarding to see that research shows what I've always believed to be true about young children and the importance of the early childhood years."

IS EARLY CHILDHOOD EDUCATION RIGHT FOR YOU?
WHAT IT TAKES TO BE AN EARLY CHILDHOOD EDUCATOR

The rewards of working in early childhood education are rich indeed, but early childhood education is not a career for everyone. First and foremost, to be an effective early childhood educator, you must truly enjoy working with children and care about their welfare. "You have to go into the field because you love this work, because you want to work with families and children," says Amy Flynn, director of the Bank Street College of Education's Bank Street Family Center in Manhattan. Juanita March, head teacher in a Reno, Nevada, daycare center, agrees: "It's not just any old job. If you don't like what you do, you are going to be doing the children in your care a real disservice. They need their time away from mom and dad to be in the care of someone who *wants* to be with them and help them grow."

Working with parents is also an important aspect of the job. "It comes with the whole package," says Flynn. As Friday puts it, early childhood educators "work as partners with parents in the education of children," and early childhood educators need to be passionate about working with the entire family unit.

To be an early childhood educator, caring about children and their families is a top priority. But that's not all it takes. Early childhood educators also share other important characteristics, including:

▶ patience
▶ flexibility
▶ creativity
▶ a nurturing, warm personality
▶ good communication skills
▶ good listening skills
▶ excellent problem-solving skills

They also:

▶ enjoy planning and organizing activities
▶ enjoy helping others discover and build their talents

▶ are good at interpreting and attending to people's emotional and physical needs

▶ enjoy challenges

▶ are passionate about giving young children a strong educational foundation and a sense of independence and self-worth

In addition, cautions Dr. Deborah Ceglowski, professor of early childhood education at the University of Minnesota in Minneapolis, it's important to be realistic about money. "To be fair to my students, one of the things I encourage them to think about is how much money they need to survive," says Ceglowski. As rich as the emotional rewards are, early childhood education is not a career for those interested in financial gain. If you have a number of major expenses, such as a mortgage or extensive student loans, you may need to supplement your income if you decide to pursue a career as an early childhood educator.

Trying It Out

One of the best ways to determine if early childhood education is right for you is to try it out by spending some time working with young children. You can get invaluable experience in early childhood education by:

- babysitting
- working as a childcare assistant at your local YMCA, YWCA, or other organization
- volunteering in the childcare center at your church or other organization
- working as a camp counselor or after-school program aide
- signing up for an early childhood education internship through your school

ENTERING THE FIELD OF EARLY CHILDHOOD EDUCATION

Because there are many different types of childcare arrangements, there are many ways to enter the field of early childhood education. You may be eligible for many positions, such as a nanny or teacher's aide, with just a high school diploma or graduate equivalency degree and little or no previous childcare experience. Other positions may require you to be a certified Child

Development Associate or Certified Childcare Professional, two certifications awarded to candidates who have a certain amount of experience in childcare and complete specific professional development requirements, or to have a college certificate or degree in early childhood education (these certification and degree programs are described in Chapter 2). Obviously, the more experience and education you have, the more job opportunities you will have because you will be eligible for more positions in more types of centers and schools.

WHAT'S IN A NAME? THE TERMINOLOGY OF EARLY CHILDHOOD CARE

Childcare center, preschool, nursery school, homecare . . . what is the difference between these types of early childhood education programs? In many ways, it is mostly a matter of hours. In a nursery school or preschool (the more common title), children typically attend for just a few hours a day (9–11:30, for example, or 12:30–3:30). Children in a childcare center or daycare, on the other hand, typically stay the bulk of the day, often eight hours or more if their parents are working full time. A homecare (also called "family childcare provider") is simply a small (typically 5–10 children) preschool or childcare run out of someone's home.

Many people have the mistaken impression that preschools prepare young children for kindergarten while childcare centers or daycares don't. But the fact is, "you can't separate the two," says Flynn. "Any good childcare program will include educational care," offering the same kind of school readiness curriculum provided in a preschool. Ceglowski agrees: "Just because it's a 'childcare center' and not a 'preschool' doesn't mean there isn't that preschool aspect. Most childcare centers have incorporated a preschool curriculum, especially in their morning routine."

KINDS OF JOBS IN EARLY CHILDHOOD EDUCATION

Classifying early childhood education positions and job titles runs a similar pattern. A "childcare worker" or "childcare provider" typically refers to someone who manages the care of children during the full working day, often eight hours or more. Their daily routine includes the teaching of a preschool curriculum as well as "regular" daycare, which includes providing meals and a period of rest for children as well as general nurturing and opportunities for social and physical development.

A "preschool teacher," on the other hand, may work an eight-hour day, but will typically work with two or three different groups of children. Many preschools, for example, have a two- or three-hour morning session and then a two- or three-hour afternoon session. They may also provide early morning care (from 8–9, for example) and/or an after-school program (from 3:00–4:30, for example) for a limited number of students. Some preschools also offer a full day program, especially for five year olds, but a full preschool day typically runs about six hours, like a regular elementary school day (for example, 8:45–3:15) rather than a typical eight-hour workday.

This general division aside, there are important differences in the kinds of positions early childhood educators may hold. Following are the most common job titles in early childhood education and a brief description of the duties and qualifications for each.

Preschool Teacher

Preschool teachers typically work with children aged three to five and usually follow a school readiness curriculum, teaching children important foundation skills such as letter recognition, phonics, number recognition, counting, and introductory writing along with basic natural science (such as the seasons, the life cycle of plants, and the weather). They develop lessons and activities that are playful yet educational. Daily activities typically include storytime and art projects, and music lessons are usually offered at least once a week. Qualifications vary, but a college degree is often required, especially for employment in a preschool in a public school system.

Childcare Provider or Childcare Worker

Childcare provider is a general term covering those who care for children in full-day childcare centers or daycare programs. For three to five year olds, their duties are similar to those of preschool teachers with the added responsibility of overall care, as childcare providers must also make sure children get adequate food and rest throughout the day. Because they have more time with children, there are often several periods of less structured, exploratory play throughout the day. Qualifications will vary depending upon the type of center or school. Most childcare providers need a minimum of several years' experience, a college certificate in early childhood education, and/or certification through a professional organization.

Nanny/Au Pair

Nannies and au pairs are childcare providers who work for individual families in their homes. They may take care of one or several children and may live with the family (au pairs) or come to the family's home only during working hours (nannies). They manage the total care of the child(ren), including feeding, nurturing, and developmental guidance. They are also often responsible for general housework, such as dishes and laundry. Some nannies and au pairs may be asked to provide specific educational services, such as teaching the child(ren) a foreign language. Nannies and au pairs may receive special training in a nanny school or may be hired simply on the basis of their natural ability to work with children and their nurturing personality.

Assistant Teacher

An assistant teacher is often a teacher in training (for example, a third-year college student) who helps a head teacher with all activities in the classroom. Assistant teachers may work full or part time and often assist in developing and implementing lessons. Qualifications will vary depending upon the amount of responsibility the assistant teacher has in the classroom.

Teacher Aide

Teacher aides are often volunteers or part-time employees who assist in the preschool or childcare center but are not necessarily training to become teachers themselves and have little responsibility with the actual instruction of students. They may help set up the classroom, assist students with an art project, read to children during circle time, or help the head teacher organize materials for the next day. Requirements are typically minimal.

Head Teacher

A head teacher is typically in charge of one or more assistant teachers and may supervise teachers in other classrooms. Head teachers are often responsible for planning and implementing the curriculum, maintaining records, and organizing staff development activities. Head teachers typically have five or more years of experience, a college degree, and continuing education credentials.

Director

Childcare center or preschool directors are the administrators who oversee the functions of the entire early childhood education program. They typically develop the curriculum, shape the school or center's philosophy, hire and train faculty and staff, handle crises, and manage the advertising, public relations, and finances of the organization. While they may have daily contact with many children and parents, unless the school or center is very small, they often spend little time actually working with children in the classroom as their other duties occupy most of their time. They are often mentors for their faculty and may have several certificates or degrees.

EARLY CHILDHOOD EDUCATION ENVIRONMENTS

Early childhood educators can work in a wide variety of settings. Nannies and au pairs, for example, typically work in the home of the child(ren) they care for; homecare providers create a childcare center or preschool in their own home; other childcare workers and preschool teachers care for children outside of their homes in daycare centers and preschools. Childcare centers and preschools come in all shapes and sizes, from a small homecare with just three or four children to a large, government-funded daycare center with eighty children. Some schools and centers are located in corporate office buildings while others are held at local community organizations such as the YMCA. This section briefly describes some of the more typical early childhood education environments.

Public versus Private Centers and Schools

Many school districts offer a year of preschool as part of their public school system program, and these preschools are open to all children within the community. In areas that do not offer pre-kindergarten classes as part of their elementary school, parents can find a large pool of private preschools to which they must apply and pay fees in order to have their children attend. Public preschools are funded by the government and must therefore follow all government guidelines and their state board of education curriculum. Private schools, on the other hand, are typically responsible for their own funding and have much greater flexibility in their curriculum and other functions. The same general distinctions are true for public vs. private childcare centers.

Chains and Franchises

While most childcare centers and preschools are either part of a public school system or independently owned and operated, an increasing number of centers and schools are franchises or chains of large, even nation-wide companies. KinderCare, for example, now has over 1,100 learning centers across the country, while Tutor Time Child Care Learning Centers has centers in 25 states as well as in Canada, Hong Kong, and Portugal. Whether a center is part of a chain (owned by the corporation) or a franchise (owned by an individual who must abide by the policies and practices of the corporation), child-care providers can expect to have detailed documentation of policies and procedures as well as a thoroughly developed curriculum to follow. Curricula and activities are usually highly structured and faculty can typically expect strong support in terms of resources, but creativity and flexibility in the classroom may be quite limited.

Religious Schools and Centers

Private schools and centers may have religious or other institutional affiliations. In a center or school affiliated with a religious organization, such as a daycare in a synagogue, teachers will often be expected to provide basic religious instruction as part of the curriculum. Books and other educational materials may revolve around religious themes and there may be greater emphasis on moral development and character education.

Corporate Childcare

Corporate daycare centers provide parents with the opportunity to be near their children in case of emergency and to visit their children periodically throughout the day. This sort of arrangement is especially beneficial to nursing mothers. While few corporations actually provide onsite childcare, those that do will typically include a preschool curriculum for the three to five year olds and the same kind of nurturing, exploratory environment found in other childcare centers.

Cooperative Childcare

Cooperative daycare centers and preschools are usually private, community-based organizations in which parents are actively involved. Parents are typically required to serve as teacher aides on a regular, rotating basis and to serve on various committees, such as curriculum development, fundraising, or facility maintenance.

Montessori Schools

Montessori schools differ from other childcare centers and preschools in that they follow the educational philosophy developed by Maria Montessori. One of Montessori's main principles is that children should be allowed to choose the kind of work they are interested in rather than following a set curriculum. For example, one child may choose to spend all morning sorting shapes and colors while another might spend his time playing with blocks and painting; they are able to pursue independent interests for much of the day. The Montessori classroom is carefully designed with educational activities spread throughout the room for children to choose. Teachers work with each child individually and in small groups to help them understand new concepts. Montessori schools also often allow children of different ages to mix in the classroom and encourage the older children to share their knowledge with their younger classmates.

Homecare

Homecare providers (also called family childcare providers) offer childcare to a small number of children in their own home. Many remodel a small section of their home to create a classroom environment and meet safety codes and licensing requirements. They may care for children of mixed ages (from birth to age six or more) or may limit their practice to children of one age group. Homecare providers have the great luxury of working in their own home and do not have to commute to work, but having a homecare has some drawbacks in the form of greater around-the-home maintenance and a highly porous division between the work and home environment.

Specialized/Recreational Programs

Before- and after-school programs, summer camps, and specialized programs for young children offer children the opportunity to engage in extracurricular activities either while parents are at work or when parents wish to provide enrichment experiences. These recreational and specialized programs may include learning a sport such as gymnastics, arts programs that introduce children to the fine or performing arts, and musical instruction. These programs may be organized by public schools, community organizations, religious institutions, or national franchises (such as KinderArt), so environments vary greatly.

AREAS OF SPECIALIZATION

As an early childhood educator, you have many choices regarding the kind of teaching and care you want to provide. As you prepare to enter the field or even after you have been working with children for several years, you can get certified and/or specialize in one or more of the following areas.

Infant and Toddler Care

Infant/toddler care specialists work with children from birth to age three. Obviously, newborns and toddlers have separate and distinct needs from the three- to five-year-olds, who typically receive the kind of school readiness curriculum that most childcare centers and preschools offer older children. Infant and toddler care specialists focus on the developmental needs of the first two years and on providing a healthy, safe, exploratory learning environment as children learn to walk and talk in their care. And infant/toddler care is a specialization that is expanding rapidly. According to Flynn, "the area of infant/toddler care is growing by leaps and bounds because more and more parents are going back to work earlier." Schools and professional organizations across the country are responding by offering more classes and professional development activities focused on the earliest years.

Special Education

Special education is another specialization experiencing rapid growth. In fact, the Bureau of Labor Statistics predicts that by the year 2005, the need for special educators in the United States will increase by a phenomenal 53%. Whether you work with special needs children in their homes, in a small day-care center, or in the pre-kindergarten class of an elementary school, this specialization will allow you to work with students with many types of disabilities and special needs, including:

- ▶ attention deficit disorder (ADD)
- ▶ autism
- ▶ blindness
- ▶ deafness
- ▶ developmental delays
- ▶ mental retardation (mild/moderate or severe/profound)
- ▶ physical disabilities
- ▶ serious emotional disturbances
- ▶ specific learning disabilities (such as dyslexia)
- ▶ speech or language impediments

According to federal law, special educators must follow an Individual Education Program (IEP), which is a written agreement between parents and the center or school describing the child's specific needs and how those needs will be addressed. But special educators maintain a certain degree of flexibility in how they implement those learning and care goals.

Even if you don't want to work exclusively with children who have special needs, Flynn recommends that all early childhood educators consider special education certification. "It will make you much more marketable and a much more well-rounded teacher," says Flynn, and because of changes in inclusion laws around the country, more and more states are requiring childcare centers and preschools to mainstream children with special needs. In Head Start schools, for example, at least 10% of the students must have special needs, and more and more schools are establishing similar policies. Besides, says Flynn, "Every teacher should know how to handle children with special needs because you are bound to have children with special needs in your classroom. And special education certification also enables you to earn a better salary."

Bilingual Education/English as a Second Language

Bilingual and English as a Second Language (ESL) teachers work with children who do not speak English. Bilingual educators are fluent in English and a second language, and they work with students in their native tongue to help them develop proficiency in English. For example, in Flushing, New York, where there is a large population of Korean immigrants, many childcare centers and preschools offer bilingual education with classes and childcare provided by Korean-speaking teachers. For more information about bilingual programs and certification, visit the National Clearinghouse for Bilingual Education at www.ncbe.gwu.edu.

ESL teachers provide a similar service with the difference that they do not necessarily speak another language and do not conduct classes in the students' native tongue. Instead, ESL educators are specially trained to teach English to students who speak any other language. Thus they might have children from a variety of countries in their class. Rebecca Wyatt, for example, teaches three year olds in a multilingual childcare center in Sacramento, California. "We have children who speak Spanish, Vietnamese, Mandarin, Hindu, and Russian," she says. "While they hear and speak these languages at home, we teach them to start speaking in English through songs, games, and of course lots of repetition. It's very rewarding to watch the children develop the ability to speak to each other and express themselves in English. And I love it when they go home and teach their parents what they've learned." For more information about ESL certification, visit the website of Teachers of English to Speakers of Other Languages, Inc., at www.tesol.org.

Foreign Language Instruction

More and more, preschools and childcare centers are offering instruction in foreign languages as part of their early childhood education curriculum. Early childhood educators who specialize in teaching languages to young children take advantage of the fact that they are in the prime developmental stage for language acquisition and can absorb a second language more easily at this age than at any other. Like ESL, foreign languages are taught through songs, games, and repetition.

Music and Arts Education

Music and art are important components of any preschool or childcare center curriculum. As a music specialist, you might introduce young children to musical instruments, teach them songs, and explore basic rhythms. Most preschools offer music instruction at least one or two days a week, and there are now many music education training programs for early childhood educators. Music Together, for example, an international music education program, offers teacher training and certification programs for early childhood educators. The National Association for the Education of Young Children (NAEYC) also offers workshops and training programs at local and national conferences. For more information about music education, visit the National Association for Music Education at www.menc.org.

Early childhood arts education follows a similar pattern. Arts specialists typically introduce children to various media, exploring basic art concepts such as color, texture, and form through drawing, painting, pottery, and other artistic formats. They also use art to teach about various cultures. Special training is available through professional organizations and college courses.

Technology

While most preschools and childcare centers offer little formal technology instruction, any expertise in technology can give you an important edge in the early childhood classroom and provide you with special career opportunities. If you are very knowledgeable about computer technology and in particular its impact on learning for young children, you may be asked to manage technology education in your center or school. This may include developing the school's technology curriculum, training your colleagues on how to use the computer, and guiding colleagues in how to best integrate technology in their classroom. You may also be asked to purchase and maintain computer hardware and software, create or maintain the school or center's website, and/or offer basic computer instruction to parents.

Childcare Directing

Many early childhood education programs offer certificates for childcare directing with classes that cover management, finances, marketing, and other aspects of running a childcare business. If you have a desire to move into an administrative position, you will be more marketable with a solid educational background in some of these areas.

SALARIES IN EARLY CHILDHOOD EDUCATION

As you are already aware, early childhood education is not a career that offers tremendous financial reward. Teachers, in general, earn low salaries, and early childhood education salaries are unfortunately at the bottom of the scale. An elementary school teacher with ten years of experience, for example, can expect to earn at least $30–35,000 per year, while an early childhood educator with ten years of experience will typically earn between $25–30,000.

It is important to remember that early childhood education salaries can range considerably and depend upon numerous factors, including the teacher's level of education and years of experience, as well as the type of school or center, its location, and the specific population it serves. A preschool teacher with a four-year degree and ten years of experience, for example, may earn close to $30,000 a year while a childcare worker who just graduated from high school and has only babysitting experience may earn less than $18,000. Similarly, a homecare provider in a wealthy suburban setting may gross over $40,000 while a homecare provider in a depressed inner city area may gross less than $20,000. And childcare providers in onsite corporate daycare centers can expect to earn more than those working in non-profit centers serving economically disadvantaged communities.

Salary Statistics: Low but Growing Wages

The Department of Labor's Bureau of Labor Statistics (BLS—www.bls.gov) reports that the median annual earnings of preschool teachers for the year 1998 was $17,310, with the salaries ranging from less than $12,000 to over $30,000. In 1997, the median annual earnings for preschool teachers in various industries were as follows:

Median Annual Earnings for Preschool Teachers, 1997

Elementary and secondary schools	$23,300
Individual and family services	$18,800
Social services, not elsewhere classified	$17,900
Civic and social associations	$17,300
Child daycare services	$15,700

These statistics show that preschool teachers, especially those in the public school system, typically earn more than childcare providers in daycare centers. It is important to note, however, that the median hourly wage for all early childhood educators has increased considerably since 1997, and while comparable statistics are not available for median annual wages for more recent years, a comparison of hourly wage figures indicate a clear upward trend:

Median hourly wages for:	1997	2000	Increase
Preschool teachers in child daycare services	$6.00	$6.74	$0.74/hr
Preschool teachers in elementary schools	$7.30	$8.56	$1.26/hr

The Center for the Childcare Workforce—a nonprofit organization dedicated to improving working conditions for early childhood educators—offers a state-by-state breakdown of the 1999 BLS wage statistics for early childhood educators at www.ccw.org/whatsnew/yourstate.html. The average hourly wage for childcare workers in New Jersey, for example, was $7.84, while preschool teachers in New Jersey earned an average of $10.62 per hour. In Idaho, one of the states offering the lowest early childhood education wages, childcare workers earned an average of $6.50 per hour and preschool teachers $7.90. Childcare workers and preschool teachers in Washington,

DC, earned the highest hourly rates in the nation, averaging $10.62 and $12.29 per hour respectively.

Teaching assistant salaries for the year 2000 averaged $17,350, according to the BLS, with wages ranging from $12,200 to $27,550.

Self-employed childcare workers can earn a range of salaries, depending upon various factors, including the number of hours worked, the number and ages of children in their care, their location, overhead costs, and the socioeconomic status of the families in the area.

Statistics indicate that **Montessori teachers** on average enjoy higher salaries than other preschool teachers. According to the North American Montessori Teachers Academy (www.montessori-namta.org), a teacher in a United States Montessori school can expect to earn a starting salary between $20–25,000. A Montessori teacher with five to ten years of experience can expect to earn between $30–35,000, while a director of a Montessori school can earn between $30–60,000 or more per year.

The International Nanny Association also reports respectable hourly wages for **nannies and au pairs**. According to their 2001 Survey of Salaries and Benefits (available at www.nanny.org), nannies earned an average hourly wage of $10.25, as much as many of the higher-paid preschool teacher salaries across the country. However, preschool teachers typically have much more comprehensive benefits than nannies, who must often pay for their own healthcare coverage.

Finally, teachers with **special education** certification can expect higher than average salaries. The BLS reports a median annual salary of $40,880 for special educators in preschools through elementary school for the year 2000, with salaries ranging from $25,000 to $65,000.

JOB OUTLOOK AND HIRING TRENDS

Despite the current recession, the job outlook for early childhood education remains strong, continuing an expansion sparked by the influx of women in the workforce in the 1970s. According to the BLS, there were about 1.2 million early childhood education full- and part-time positions held in the year 2000 in the following industries:

40%	Self-employed (homecare providers, nannies, and owners/directors)
12%	Employed by childcare centers and preschools
3%	Employed by religious institutions

The remaining 45% were employed by community organizations, in state and local government, private households, and corporate onsite childcare centers, though only a very small percentage of private corporations offer onsite childcare.

(Source: www.bls.gov/oco/ocos170.htm—12/30/01)

Improving the Status of Early Childhood Educators

Of the many early childhood education professional organizations, the mission of the nonprofit Council for Professional Recognition (CPR) is to improve the status of early childhood educators by "professionalizing" the field, set standards (the "CDA Competency Standards"), and award the Child Development Associate credential to early childhood educators who complete the CPR's one-year training program. For more information, see Chapter 2 or visit the CPR's website at www.cdacouncil.org.

The good news for those interested in becoming early childhood educators is that the number of jobs for early childhood educators is expected to continue to grow. According to the BLS's *Occupational Outlook Handbook*, "Employment of childcare workers is projected to increase about as fast as the average for all occupations through the year 2010." Despite demographic changes (the BLS predicts little increase, if any, in the number of childbearing women in the labor force, for example), "the number of children under five years of age is expected to rise gradually over the projected 2000–10 period," and "[t]he proportion of youngsters enrolled full or part time in childcare and preschool programs is likely to continue to increase, spurring demand for additional childcare workers."

Three key factors are responsible for this trend. First is the growing acknowledgment of the importance of early childhood education. As more studies show the impact that quality early childhood education has on children, more government, public, and private funding has become available for early childhood education programs, and more parents are receiving subsidies so that they can enroll their children in programs they might not otherwise be able to afford. "There has been a dramatic increase in state support of early childhood education in the last decade," says Professor Ceglowski. "States are committed to creating programs for young children beyond already existing childcare centers."

More Children in Childcare

The Work and Families Institute's *1997 National Study of the Changing Workforce* reports the following trends that have helped spur the growth of the early childhood education industry:

- a marked increase (from 66% to 78%) in the last 20 years in the number of families in which both partners are employed
- a sharp increase in the last 20 years in the number of workers raising children alone (nearly one in five employed parents is single)
- approximately one-third of employed parents with pre-kindergarten children rely on non-family arrangements (nannies, childcare centers, and preschools) for childcare

Second is the corresponding increase in education and training required for early childhood educators. As people begin to take early childhood education more seriously and see it as much more than just "babysitting" while mom and dad are at work, more parents are seeking childcare providers with higher qualifications to nurture their children. Twenty years ago, for example, there were just a handful of nanny schools and training programs. Now, the National Association of Nannies (www.nannyassociation.com) lists 22 colleges and nanny training schools across the country, and many parents now hire only Certified Professional Nannies. Similarly, teachers in the National Head Start program will soon be required to have at least a two-year associate degree in order to be employed.

The third factor is the increased expectations for children entering kindergarten. "Children are expected to have some previous school experience" by the time they enter kindergarten, says Flynn, and to have developed some basic academic skills through that schooling. Many parents worry that if their children don't attend preschool, they will enter kindergarten already a year behind their classmates. "Kids are learning so much in preschool these days," says Christina Lee, mother of four-year-old twins in Pittsburgh, Pennsylvania. "I don't want my children to have to play catch-up when they get to kindergarten. I'm worried that it will damage their self-esteem and make them dislike school. Enrolling them in preschool gives me the security that they will be on par with, or maybe even ahead of, their peers, that they're comfortable with a school environment, and that they will continue to enjoy learning."

A BRIGHT FUTURE

For these reasons and more, while other industries are cutting back and laying off employees, the field of early childhood education is enjoying a period of growth that is expected to continue well into the next decade. It is a great time to become an early childhood educator.

THE INSIDE TRACK

Who: Carolyn Hanson

What: Preschool Teacher

Where: Las Vegas, NV

INSIDER'S STORY

My first teaching position after finishing graduate school was at a small private nursery
school, where I cotaught three- and four-year-olds with a woman who had been
teaching there for many years. Working in a classroom along with an experienced
teacher was an invaluable experience for me because she helped me learn how to
deal with the highly-charged, emotional atmosphere of the classroom. I have always
loved young children and after working as a camp counselor and babysitter during high
school and college, I knew I wanted to be a teacher. However, nothing can really
prepare you for the enormous task of educating children in this age group. Teaching
preschoolers demands a great deal of patience as well as an understanding of the way
a young child's mind works. For many children, their preschool teacher is the first adult
authority figure they have encountered other than their parents, and this new
relationship can often be a struggle for the child, particularly if he or she is nervous
about starting school. As a new teacher, I often found it difficult to establish myself as
an effective authority figure, particularly if a child was upset and looking to me for
emotional support, or trying to test my limits as a disciplinarian.

Three- and four-year-olds can be unpredictable and experience sudden mood
swings that can be unsettling to a new teacher. One moment, they're all playing quietly
in small groups; in the next second, three of them are fighting over a toy, two others
are asking loudly about snack time, and another child is running around in circles
wildly. My first instinct in such situations was to raise my voice in order to gain control
of the room, but this often aggravated the problem by making the children more
excitable. My colleague, on the other hand, was able to restore order by speaking to
the children in a calm but firm tone, often using a game or song to bring the group
together and quiet them down. In cases where a child was hurt or upset, she taught
me the importance of remaining calm and, above all, not over-reacting. I learned
quickly that teaching this age group is an extremely physical job—from running around
the classroom to comforting crying children, I found myself constantly on the move. My
first few weeks at the school were exhausting.

However, I realized quickly that despite the hard work, teaching preschool is an extremely rewarding job. One of the best things about working with three- and four-year-olds is their excitement about learning. In a sense, a child entering school for the first time is a blank slate, and so in teaching my students the most basic skills, I feel that I am making a real impact on their lives—it's thrilling to watch their development. In another sense, of course, each child is already a highly individual human being with a distinct personality, and it is fascinating to watch these personalities grow and interact with each other. Finally, one of the best aspects of working with young children is their infinite affection and loyalty—at the end of a particularly hard day, it's always gratifying to get hugs and smiles from my students.

I think that the most important skills to learn when working with young children, apart from patience, are flexibility and a great deal of energy. Preschoolers have a great capacity to learn, but also have a very short attention span. A teacher needs to be thinking and reacting constantly; if the students begin to show signs of restlessness with one activity, it's time to move on to another. There is very little down time during the day, even when the children are eating or playing independently, and this is important to consider if you are a person who needs a certain amount of quiet time during the workday. Being sensitive to the psychology of this age group is also essential; trying to use adult logic to reason with a four-year-old usually results in frustration on both sides. Finally, it's important to have a healthy sense of humor, particularly since nothing will ever go completely as planned when you're dealing with very young children! Often, the surprises children present us with can be learning experiences in themselves.

CHAPTER two

ALL ABOUT EARLY CHILDHOOD EDUCATION PROGRAMS

IN THIS chapter you will find out how to pick an education program and an institution that is right for you. You will also read about different certificates and degrees that are available (including associate, bachelor's, and graduate), what the programs leading to those qualifications offer in terms of courses and employment opportunities upon graduation, how to get into them, and how to succeed.

CHILDCARE IS a great profession for those who love kids. But while loving kids is a necessary element of a successful career in childcare, it is not sufficient. The number of parents of young children who need to work at least part time is increasing and as a result, there is a higher demand for quality professional childcare, according to the *Occupational Outlook Handbook*. Trained individuals are needed to serve as teacher aides and assistants, preschool teachers, private childcare and daycare employees, and special education assistants.

Preschool children have an amazing potential to learn and develop and can greatly benefit from the guidance of an educated and experienced childcare professional. Making sure a child is fed, changed, and not crying is not enough. Parents expect to see their children learn and develop new skills and engage in constructive play at their daycare centers and preschools. Managing a classroom full of kids can be fun, but is by no means an easy job. Getting all children to cooperate and to learn requires knowledge and practice. You can get both by obtaining a certificate or a degree in early childhood education. The question is: what kind of program is right for you?

CHOOSING THE RIGHT PROGRAM

What kind of program is best for you depends on what education you have had up until now, what kind of job you are hoping to get when you complete the program, what you hope to learn from your program, and how much time and money you are willing to invest in your education. Are you just finishing high school? Are you currently working with children and would like to get additional formal education? Do you have a degree in another field and would like to change your career and become an early childhood educator? Do you already have a college degree in early childhood education but would like to learn more or get into a different aspect of early childhood, such as program directing, or special education?

If you are still in high school or just starting out in early childhood education, your idea of what you would like to do after your studies may not be very clear. The following quiz should help you develop a greater sense of your own interests, whether you are just beginning your career, or pursuing professional development in early childhood education. Try to answer the following questions, to get a general sense of the direction you want to take.

- ▶ What age group would you like to work with?
- ▶ What kind of setting would you like to work in (small/large, private/ public, urban/suburban, special needs, diverse background, or Montessori)?
- ▶ What position would you like to ultimately hold (assistant teacher/ teacher/family childcare provider/parent educator/program director)?
- ▶ How much time can you, or are you willing to, spend in school (total number of months/years)?
- ▶ How much can you afford to spend for your education? (Remember that financial aid is available for most programs. See Chapter 3 for information on financial aid.)

▶ What do you hope to learn?

▶ How flexible is your schedule? Can you attend classes during the day? Or do you need to attend only in the evening? Are you willing to take classes online?

▶ Are you willing to travel or relocate?

The Knowledge You Will Gain

Make a list of subjects (courses) you would like to cover. For example, would you like to learn effective classroom management techniques? Are you interested in getting instruction on developing an effective curriculum for toddlers? In other words, if you could create a program, what would it be like? Then compare this ideal program to existing programs that you can apply to. Typical courses will include Child Development, Curriculum Planning, Parent Relations, Class Management, Creative Activities for Children, and Safe Environments for Children. You will probably get the most satisfaction out of a program that focuses on the topics you would like to learn more about. The philosophy or goals of the program should appeal to you and should be compatible with your own teaching style.

The Jobs Available after Completion of Program

Find out what jobs and positions would be available to you when you complete a particular program and make sure that it is what you want before you apply. One way to do this is to look at advertisements for positions in early childhood education and find out what the requirements are for the kind of positions you would be interested in. Or, you can ask the program director of the institution you plan to work in what kind of jobs you would be qualified for if you were to complete the program you are interested in. The third way is to talk to individuals in the field who already hold the positions you would like to have and find out what their educational background is. Keep in mind that standards are increasing and that what was considered sufficient education for a position 20 years ago may not suffice today. But generally, a professional in the field will be able to point you in the right direction.

The Time for Completion

Programs in early childhood education can last anywhere from a couple of weeks for some certificates to a few years (to get a college or graduate degree). When considering application to a program, find out whether you will be able to get certified in the state you plan to work in, whether you will be qualified for the type of position in which you are interested and whether you will gain the knowledge you are looking for.

If you are not sure that this field is right for you, you can explore your options by taking a few education classes at a community college or getting a certificate. (Learn more about certificate and degree programs starting on page 34.) Be sure to find out if the credits you complete at a shorter program could be transferred to a four-year school if you decide to stick with early childhood education.

The amount of time you can spend on your education also depends on your current family and financial situation. If you are working or taking care of your own children, it may be difficult to go to daytime classes. But you could still look into evening or distance learning programs or you could attend part time, whether it is during the day, over the Internet, or in the evening. Then, you need to search for schools where class scheduling is more flexible.

CHOOSING THE RIGHT COLLEGE OR INSTITUTION

Once you have decided what kind of certificate or degree you would like to obtain (see pages 26–27 to help you decide which program is right for you), you still need to find schools or institutions where the program in which you are interested is offered and then choose a few schools that you would like to attend, if you are accepted. You should consider:

- ▶ the academic strength of the program
- ▶ the location and size of the institution
- ▶ the cost and flexibility of the program
- ▶ the admission requirements
- ▶ the career services at the institution
- ▶ the quality of the faculty

Academics

The academic strength of the program should be your number-one criterion when choosing a school, because the curriculum is the reason you are enrolling—to learn more about early childhood education. Check whether the program you plan to attend is accredited and by which agency. An agency grants accreditation to a program that fulfills specific minimum academic requirements. Anybody can issue you a piece of paper that says you have graduated from an early childhood program and that you are qualified to work as a childcare professional and call it a diploma. But if the diploma is issued by an accredited program, it carries weight and credibility. Also, find out whether the completion of the program leads to state certification in early childhood education. If you are planning to pursue a certificate or complete a two-year program, check whether the credits you earn could be applied toward a four-degree program if you decide to continue your education.

Find out about the reputation or ranking of the program. A renowned program will attract top students and faculty and may offer more research or internship opportunities. But that doesn't mean that a small community college doesn't have a great program. A bigger and renowned school will have more resources, but it also might be more expensive. What you learn and get out of your studies depends primarily on you, so not being in a renowned program doesn't mean you won't be successful, or that your education will not be valuable.

Are courses you are interested in offered at that school? Shawn Severin, who graduated from North Seattle Community College, is very satisfied with their Early Childhood Education program. "I continue to teach at a large, private preschool and feel my success in this field is largely due to having received my education there. I continue to utilize the materials I developed in my classes, refer to a wealth of articles supplied by my instructors, and put to use specific techniques and curriculum ideas I was exposed to at North Seattle."

Location

The location of the school or institution you consider attending will be a factor in determining whether you will finally apply or not. How far are you willing to commute? Are you willing to move? How important is it to you to be close to family and friends? Do you prefer attending a program in an urban or suburban setting? Both settings have advantages and disadvantages. Suburban schools usually have a campus that is self-contained. The students have more opportunity to interact, since most live on-campus or close to the campus. But outside of the suburban campus, there may be very little going on. A school in a city can be more dynamic, the population is likely to be more diverse, and there will be more opportunity to socialize outside of the school setting. In an urban school there are also more internship opportunities in daycare and preschool settings. However, if you are used to or prefer being in a quiet place, closer to nature, you may not enjoy an urban campus. Similarly, if you are used to or like the hustle and bustle of a city, the countryside or suburbia could bore you. Even if you have made the country/city decision, make sure you visit the neighborhood where the school is located. Is it safe? Would you feel comfortable walking on or near campus after an evening class?

Size

The size of the school is not a big deciding factor for everyone. However, some could be intimidated in large schools and crowded classes. You may prefer small classes where the faculty to student ratio is high and you receive a lot of individual attention. At a small school you will have the advantage of quickly getting to know other students. On the other hand, you may prefer the large classes where you can maintain some anonymity and have a greater number of peers to socialize with or work with on group projects. A large school is also more likely to offer a greater variety of classes, taught by more faculty members.

The size of the early education program at the school is also a factor you need to consider. Just because a school is large doesn't mean that there are many students who are majoring in early childhood education. Again, there are pros and cons to attending a large program. For example, if the program is large, more classes will be offered, the library will hold more literature and journals of interest to you, you will network with more students with the same interests, and there will be more internships available through the school. But the classes may be more crowded, you will be competing with more students for the same internships, and you may miss out on the personal attention you would get in a smaller program.

Distance Learning

In a distance learning program, a student learns from materials supplied over the Internet or through instructional tapes and notes sent by mail, without having to physically go to class. Distance learning has the obvious advantage that a student can take a course from miles away and learn valuable lessons in early childhood education, without leaving home. The obvious disadvantage is that there is less contact with faculty and other students than in a traditional program.

Graduate programs are more likely to be distance learning. However, some undergraduate programs that are not completely long distance may offer just a few classes online. An ideal time to experience distance learning is when you are taking classes for professional development. If you are at the point of taking professional development classes, chances are that you already have experience in the early childhood education field and that you will be able to connect the information you obtain in the distance learning educational materials with real situations that come up in childcare.

CARE Courses (www.carecourses.com) is a correspondence school for child care providers. The courses can be used to get CDA—Child Development Associate Credential—or CCP—Certified Childcare Professional Credential. All of the correspondence courses are in book format and are supplied through the mail. If you plan to use the courses you take with CARE toward a degree or for licensing purposes, make sure beforehand that you can get credit and that your state will accept the courses you take through long-distance learning for license renewal or as a fulfillment of professional development requirements.

Cost and Program Flexibility

Let's face it. Cost is an issue. Even when you get a job in early childhood education, chances are you will not be making millions of dollars, so you probably can't afford to take out too many loans to attend an early childhood education program. Pick schools that you can afford and the schools from which you are likely to get financial aid. You should also consider whether the institution is public or private. Public schools usually cost less. If the school is private, does it have a religious affiliation with which you are comfortable? Will you be able to attend in the evenings or part time if you are working full time or taking care of your own children during the day? Is distance learning available?

Tips for Choosing the School That Is Right for You

- Talk to current students. Ask about the curriculum, as well as what they like and dislike about the program and the school.
- Talk to alumni employed in early childhood education.
- Talk to faculty at the school about the program and their own interests in education.
- Sit in on a class.
- If there is a daycare center with which the institution is affiliated, ask if you can take a tour or spend some time observing classes.

Admission Requirements

Before applying to a program, check to see what the admission requirements are. Can you fulfill them? Have you completed the required education and taken the required exams? Guidance counselors often suggest applying to at least one "safety school"—a school where you have a very high chance of getting in, meaning that your academic record, test scores, or experience surpass those of the average student admitted to that school.

Requirements will vary depending upon which type of degree or certificate you choose to pursue. Some certificate programs only require a high school diploma, some experience, or recommendations. Most two- and four-year programs require a high school diploma or General Equivalency Diploma (GED). In addition, most four-year programs require standardized test scores, recommendations, and in some cases, an essay. International students at all levels, who are not native speakers of English, are required to take the Test of English as a Foreign Language (TOEFL) exam. Admission requirements for a graduate degree are typically a four-year degree, not necessarily in the childhood education field, Graduate Record Exam (GRE) scores, recommendations, an essay, and, in some cases, experience in the field. How you have done in the past academically will also determine whether you gain acceptance to a program, especially if the program is renowned.

Career Services and the Faculty

Find out if there is a career service office at the school you would like to apply to. How much help does the office offer students in searching for jobs, and building resume and interviewing skills? How many graduates of the program find employment shortly after graduating? Does the office constantly receive new job listings? How are students alerted to these listings? Does the office help students find internships and summer jobs in the early childhood field? Try to talk to at least some of the faculty. Find out what their philosophy and educational background is. Do they have a great deal of field experience? What teaching methods do they use?

Making the Most of Your Study

- Take your work seriously.
- Attend all classes.
- Complete all assignments.
- Look for ways to do more than is expected of you.
- Collect material for your portfolio (a collection of your work that is a record of accomplishments for potential employers).

PRACTICAL TRAINING

No matter how well you do in class and how wonderful your understanding of child development is, you need to apply your theoretical knowledge in order to become an effective teacher of young children. Learning to take care of kids is like learning to swim. You learn and improve the more you do it. No theory can account for the behavior and personality of each child. The only way to get comfortable working with children is to be around them as much as possible and to observe and imitate those who are good at taking care of children already. That is why almost all good programs in early childhood education include an internship or practical training component. Before graduating, students are placed in a childcare or school setting as an apprentice to more experienced teachers. Some institutions that offer early childhood degrees or certificates even have on-site centers or schools in which students of early childhood education programs can train.

Making the Most of the Practical Training

- Have a positive attitude toward the job.
- Look at your supervisor's criticism as an opportunity to improve your job skills.
- Take note of effective strategies used by your coworkers and supervisors.
- Observe coworkers' strategies that don't seem to be effective and think of different ways to handle similar situations.
- Establish a good relationship with the parents.
- Network—collect names and numbers of your colleagues.
- Collect material for your portfolio—for example, take pictures (or have someone else take pictures) of yourself working with the students, or keep samples of successful projects you led in class.

CERTIFICATES

Some certificate programs are just a collection of several classes that could be completed in a few months. Others require a whole year for completion. Depending on the state and the structure of the program, a certificate may or may not lead to state certification. And whether you can get state certification or not will depend on what kind of job you will be able to get. The requirement for enrollment in certificate programs is generally a high school diploma, but professional development certificate programs may require prior experience in the field and recommendations.

There are a variety of certificates in early childhood education. For example, West Valley College in Saratoga, CA offers the following certificate programs:

► General Early Childhood Education
► Early Childhood Program Director
► Infant-Toddler Childcare
► Parent Education Certificate
► School Age Childcare

Before you enroll in any program, you should also check whether the certificate you plan to get will count toward a college degree, if you think that you may, at some point, want to complete one. Whether the credits will count depends on what kind of certificate you get and which college you will attend. For example, a short Certificate in Infant and Toddler Care at Bellevue Community College, located in Bellevue, WA (www.bcc.ctc.edu/ece/ShortCert.html), requires the completion of only 18 credits, which can count toward a college degree. It consists of the following courses:

► Child Development (3 credits)
► Fundamentals of Early Childhood Education (5 credits)
► Infant and Toddler Care (2 credits)
► Parent Involvement (5 credits)
► Child Health and Safety (3 credits)

Great Basin College in Elko, NV offers a one-year Early Childhood Education Certificate. The college has a daycare facility for 130 children, where students enrolled in the early childhood education programs at Great Basin receive training and practical experience. The minimum requirements for degree completion are completing courses in:

► Parent/Caregiver Relationships
► Observation Skills
► Introduction to Teaching the Young Child
► Child Abuse and Neglect
► Infectious Diseases and First Aid
► The Exceptional Child
► Principles of Child Guidance
► Preschool Practicum: Early Childhood Lab
► Preschool Curriculum

▶ Individual and the Family
▶ Technical Communications
▶ Fundamentals of Speech
▶ Elementary Accounting

And one of the following:

▶ Human Relations for Teachers
▶ Psychology of Human Relations
▶ Personnel Administration

Many programs in early childhood education programs lead to the Child Development Associate (CDA) credential, awarded by the National Council for Early Childhood Professional Recognition. To receive the credential, you must complete at least 120 hours of formal education. There are over 100,000 CDA certified professionals across the nation. Most schools offering the credential training are two-year colleges or universities. Eighty-eight percent of those offering CDA training also offer college credit for CDA coursework.

The National Child Care Association (NCCA) awards the Certified Child Care Professional (CCP) credential. One of the requirements for attaining the credential is to complete 180 clock hours of education and training for professional development. Another requirement is a four-month experience in a licensed early childhood facility. Anyone who is at least 18 years old and makes the commitment to fulfill the requirements is eligible for the credential. Pursuing this credential cost $475, but scholarships are available from NCCA.

Consider Becoming a Nanny

If you can see yourself as Mary Poppins, or Maria from *The Sound of Music,* even Mrs. Doubtfire to some extent, consider being a nanny. Contrary to a common misconception, a nanny is different from a babysitter. The responsibility of a nanny is to educate the children, to engage them in stimulating age-appropriate activities, to organize play-dates, to take the children to any classes or lessons they participate in, and to pay taxes. Nannies are not responsible for housework that is not child related.

In fact, the work of a nanny is very similar to the work of a preschool teacher, but for only one family.

Many nannies live with the families they work for, and travel with the family on vacation. They can get from $300 to $1000 per week depending on their education, experience and the family they work for. In addition, nannies sometimes get health insurance and usually get two weeks of vacation per year.

Although anyone who finishes high school could be a nanny, many families prefer to hire someone who has been educated to work with children and for whom childcare is a profession, rather than a temporary job. One way to become a professional nanny is to go to a nanny school.

"The school has so many interesting courses which include everything from pediatric dentistry to martial arts! It is my hope that I will be able to learn many new childcare and educating skills through this school. After 12 weeks of class and the nine-month externship, I will get my CPN - Certified Professional Nanny. The school has a placement department that helps me negotiate salaries, benefits, etc., with the families that I am interested in," said Krista Harper, a student at the English Nanny & Governess School (www.nanny-governess.com).

Find out more about becoming and being a nanny at www.nanny.org and www.nwnanny.com

ASSOCIATE DEGREES

The Associate of Applied Science Degree (A.A.S.) and Associate of Arts Degree (A.A.) in early childhood education can be obtained typically in two years by completing 60–90 credits, including field experience (practicum). They prepare students for employment in childcare, including childcare centers, Head Start programs, early childhood education programs, child welfare service agencies, and public school aid programs. They also prepare students to train other staff who work in these settings.

There are more institutions in the United States offering associate's degrees (57%) in early childhood programs than there are bachelor's degree programs (40%) offering early childhood programs. Additionally, in response to the government push to improve the quality of early childhood education staff, Head Start has mandated that 50% of program staff must have at least an associate's degree by 2003.

Most associate's degree programs include some general courses, courses specific to early childhood education, and practical training. Borough of Manhattan Community College, for example, offers an A.A.S. degree in early childhood education. The program requirements include general courses in English, mathematics, music or art, science, social science, foreign language, health education, and the following classes in early childhood education:

▶ The Exceptional Child
▶ Curriculum and Program Planning
▶ Early Childhood Education (Practicum)
▶ Curriculum and Program Planning II
▶ Supervised Instructional Experience with Infants and Toddlers (Practicum)

Common admission requirements to associate degree programs in early childhood education are a high school or GED, a 2.0–2.5 or better high school academic average, (or a comparable average for students transferring from other post-high school programs), and, in some cases, test results from ACT or SAT.

BACHELOR OF ARTS (B.A.) OR BACHELOR OF SCIENCE (B.S.) DEGREES

Some four-year colleges offer degrees (B.A. or B.S.) in early childhood education. These programs typically require completion of at least 120 credits. Early childhood education can usually be a major or a minor, but in any case, students are required to take some core courses in general education (English, mathematics, history, and so on.). With a four-year college degree, you usually have more chance for career advancement—a B.A. or B.S. will qualify you for most jobs in early childhood education.

Students at Worcester State College, in Worcester, MA, must complete the following courses in their major:

▶ Early Childhood Education Today
▶ Young Children, Learning, and Special Needs

- ▶ Curriculum and Evaluation in Early Childhood Education
- ▶ ECE Multiculturalism and Social Studies
- ▶ ECE Math
- ▶ ECE Science
- ▶ Early Literacy, Children's Literature, Language Arts
- ▶ Integrated Early Childhood Education
- ▶ Student Teaching in Early Childhood Education

In addition, they must take 60 credits of core courses, (such as English and public speaking, general education courses, language development courses, or child psychology), and complete a student teaching practicum.

Admission requirements vary from program to program, but generally, candidates should have a strong high school record, respectable SAT or ACT scores, letters of recommendation, and in many cases a college essay. Transferring from a two-year program is, in many cases, possible as well.

MONTESSORI TRAINING

Montessori childhood centers endorse the philosophies of Dr. Maria Montessori, best summarized in the motto "Help me do it by myself." Children in a Montessori setting are grouped so that the younger ones learn from the older ones, and the older ones learn by teaching the younger; each child learns at his or her own pace. The emphasis is on collaboration, rather than competition. Children are encouraged to work freely and to explore their environment, with the goal of building self-confidence and fostering independence. The salaries in a Montessori setting are often well above the average salaries in early childhood education. Benefits are also often generous, sometimes including funding for professional development and sabbaticals.

Association Montessori Internationale (AMI) training is often a requirement for working in a Montessori setting. While AMI training is preferred, a school may hire candidates who don't have a Montessori background, but are committed to the Montessori philosophy and are willing to be trained. Post Oak School in Houston, Texas recently posted a job advertisement for candidates willing to pursue Montessori training, paid for by the Post Oak School.

Montessori certification programs accept applicants who already have a college degree. Becoming a Montessori educator can take several years if you are just out of high school. The AMI certified curriculum is a one-year intensive program. A typical week of classes during a lecture session includes child development, Montessori curriculum and methods, hands-on time with the Montessori materials, and opportunities for questions and discussion. Observation training and practice teaching are also required, as is the production of your own Material Reference Books.

SPECIAL EDUCATION

The field of Early Childhood Special Education is growing. As inclusion programs become widespread, more caregivers will find it necessary to gain the knowledge to provide an optimal environment for children with special needs. While all students of early childhood education need some training to understand the issues that face special-needs children and their families, some students choose to specialize in this area. You can usually start a career in special education by taking it as a minor or attending a certificate program. Graduate degrees in Early Childhood Special Education are also available. The George Washington University School of Education and Human Development offers a Masters of Arts in this field. It includes instruction on:

▶ development of children with disabilities
▶ formal and informal assessment
▶ curricular and material development
▶ behavior management—theories and strategies
▶ family dynamics and consultation skills
▶ legal and ethical issues and public policy concerns related to children with disabilities
▶ application of classroom theory to children with special needs

GRADUATE DEGREES

Some employers prefer candidates who have, or are working toward, a master's degree. Nonetheless, if after finishing a four-year program you are still eager to learn, a graduate degree may be right for you. Or, if you have decided to change careers, you may want to complete a graduate program to gain the skills necessary to teach in the early childhood setting. One of the benefits of obtaining a graduate degree is that your salary is likely to increase with your qualifications.

To be admitted to an Early Childhood Master's Degree Program, students typically need:

- ▶ A bachelor's degree from an accredited college or university
- ▶ An acceptable grade point average in undergraduate coursework
- ▶ An acceptable score on the Miller's Analogies Test (MAT) or the GRE
- ▶ Related professional experience
- ▶ A personal interview with the program staff
- ▶ Letters of recommendation
- ▶ Copies of any teaching certificates the applicant holds
- ▶ An essay that states the applicant's purpose in undertaking graduate study

Become a Program Director

There are many roads to becoming a program director—from gaining experience as a teacher and working your way up by taking on more responsibility to starting your own daycare center. The benefits of being a program director should be apparent. You will have more opportunity to create a stimulating environment for the children, hire and develop new staff members, organize special events, and purchase new equipment. However, don't think that as the "boss" you will have more free time. On the contrary, you'll work more, worry more, solve problems that you otherwise wouldn't have to deal with, and unless you are working at a large daycare center where there is a business manager, you will have to take care of contracts and finances, which means you'll spend less time interacting with children. Rather than hoping that you will pick up the necessary skills that a good director should have on the job, consider taking classes in early childhood education program directing. National-Louis University, in Chicago, offers courses leading to Masters in Education for those who wish to become more effective program directors. Relevant classes include:

- Strategies for Supervision and Staff Development
- Financial and Legal Aspects of Child Care Management
- Technology in Child Care Administration
- Grant writing and Fundraising for Early Childhood Programs
- Public Relations and Marketing of Early Childhood Programs
- Implementing a Family Responsive Program

STATE LICENSES

Because the impact of a teacher on a child can be immense, each state in the United States sets its own teacher licensure requirements to ensure that every teacher comes to the classroom with a certain level of competence in educational methods, teaching skills, and classroom management abilities. Obtaining a state license is therefore well worth your time. Different states have different requirements for different positions in early childhood education. In California, for example, a preschool teacher must have a high school diploma (or courses leading to) and 12 units of state-approved study in Early Childhood Education. In Massachusetts, Provisional Certification with Advanced Standing is achieved at the bachelor's level. Standard Certification comes with completion of a master's degree. Students must also pass a two-part examination in order to be certified.

To find out what the requirements are in your state, check with your own state's department of education. A list of websites and contact information is available at www.recruitingteachers.org/doe.html. Look at the website for your state to find out what requirements you need to fulfill.

Now that you have a better idea of what programs are out there and where you can get more information on the programs you are interested in, get to work and fill out those applications! You are on the road to becoming a more qualified childcare professional. Chapter 3 will provide you with the information you need to know to finance your education.

THE INSIDE TRACK

Who:	Jennifer Sager
What:	Kindergarten Teacher
Where:	Whitehouse, Ohio

INSIDER'S STORY

I have always enjoyed working with children, especially young children. My mother used to teach preschool and her stories about her job always interested me. I am fascinated by the way young children learn. Being in the world of a five-year-old is truly amazing—they are able to process new information so quickly. I knew I would enjoy being the person who was able to facilitate their knowledge experience. In college, I worked for the YMCA in a daycare setting, and now I teach kindergarten in a public school.

My undergraduate experience paved the way for my career. In addition to my job teaching in daycare, I was able to teach in a school setting early on, as well as complete my method teaching in a variety of settings. My student teaching experience was split between kindergarten and second grade, each for eight weeks. This allowed me to understand how each level functioned and differed.

I received my first head teacher job the summer after I graduated. I am fortunate enough to work for an awesome school district with a super staff. My transition into the "real" teaching world was made easier with the mentoring program the district utilized. My most helpful resource has been the kindergarten teachers who have taught for many years at my school prior to me. They are very willing to share ideas, which they know will benefit our students. Once I knew the objectives for the subject areas and saw how my students were able to learn, I began to come up with many ideas on my own.

One of the biggest challenges of my job is helping young children adjust to their first formal year of schooling. Early childhood learning outcomes are geared more toward academics today than in years past. If children are not developmentally ready for the material, they tend to struggle. Early childhood educators are also usually the first to discover learning difficulties, attention disorders, and behavior problems. It is important to help parents understand and come to grips with any issues that arise when their child begins attending school for the first time.

That said, I think that teaching is the most rewarding career a person can choose! Helping a child learn to read and write is so exciting. I enjoy experiencing a young child's insights into the world around them and seeing their faces light up when they comprehend new information. My students make me smile each and every day with their funny comments and five-year-old insights on the world. I especially enjoy meeting with parents and hearing how happy and excited their children are about school. I always receive nice notes from both parents and students, who make me feel like I really am making a difference in their lives. My students from previous years come to my classroom each morning to give me a hug and say hello. It is nice to still be important in those students' lives.

As a new teacher, tap into all the resources available to you. Curriculum materials adopted by the school district contain detailed lesson plans, but search the Web for resources, use teacher resource books with ideas for all subject areas, subscribe to teacher magazines—all these channels always have fantastic activities proven helpful to teachers. My favorite kindergarten magazine also maintains a website with reproducible worksheets and activities to accompany thematic units. I have also found professional seminars for teachers beneficial. Most important, before you take on a new job, ask about mentors—experienced teachers are usually your best sources of information. Remember, they have been doing the job for years . . . they have probably picked up some tricks of the trade over the course of their careers.

CHAPTER three

FINANCIAL AID FOR THE TRAINING AND CERTIFICATION YOU NEED

IN CHAPTER 2 you learned how to find and succeed in the right training program for you. This chapter explains some of the many different types of financial aid available, gives you information on what records you will need to gather to apply for financial aid, and helps you through the process of applying for financial aid. (A sample financial aid form is included in Appendix C.) At the end of the chapter are listed many more resources that can help you find the aid you need.

YOU HAVE DECIDED on a career and you've chosen a training program. Now, you need a plan to finance your training. Perhaps you or your family has been saving for your education, and you've got the money to pay your way. However, if you're like most students, you don't have enough to cover the cost of the training program you'd like to attend. Be assured that it is likely that you can qualify for some sort of financial aid, even if you plan to attend school only part-time.

Because there are many types of financial aid, and the millions of dollars given away or loaned are available through so many sources, the process of finding funding for your education can seem confusing. Read through this chapter carefully, and check out the many resources, including websites and publications, listed in Appendix B. You will have a better understanding of where to look for financial aid, what you can qualify for, and how and when to apply.

Also take advantage of the financial aid office at the school you've chosen, or your guidance counselor if you're still in high school. These professionals can offer plenty of information, and can help to guide you through the process. If you're not in school, and haven't chosen a program yet, check the Internet. It's probably the best source for up-to-the-minute information, and almost all of it is free. There are a number of great sites at which you can fill out questionnaires with information about yourself and receive lists of scholarships and other forms of financial aid for which you may qualify. You can also apply for some types of federal and state aid online—you can even complete the Free Application for Federal Student Aid (FAFSA), the basic form that determines federal and state financial aid eligibility, online if you choose.

SOME MYTHS ABOUT FINANCIAL AID

The subject of financial aid is often misunderstood. Here are three of the most common myths:

Myth #1: All the red tape involved in finding sources and applying for financial aid is too confusing for me.
Fact: The whole financial aid process is a set of steps that are ordered and logical. Besides, several sources of help are available. To start, read this chapter carefully to get a helpful overview of the entire process and tips on how to get the most financial aid. Then, use one or more of the resources listed within this chapter and in the appendices for additional help. If you believe you will be able to cope with your training program, you will be able to cope with looking for the money to finance it—especially if you take the process one step at a time in an organized manner.

Myth #2: For most students, financial aid just means getting a loan and going into heavy debt, which isn't worth it, or working while in school, which will lead to burnout and poor grades.
Fact: Both the federal government and individual schools award grants and scholarships, which the student doesn't have to pay back. It is also possible to

get a combination of scholarships and loans. It's worth taking out a loan if it means attending the program you really want to attend, rather than settling for your second choice or not pursuing a career in your chosen field at all. As for working while in school, it's true that it is a challenge to hold down a full-time or even part-time job while in school. However, a small amount of work-study employment (10–12 hours per week) has been shown to actually improve academic performance, because it teaches students important time-management skills.

Myth #3: I can't understand the financial aid process because of all the unfamiliar terms and strange acronyms that are used.
Fact: While you will encounter an amazing number of acronyms and some unfamiliar terms while applying for federal financial aid, you can refer to the acronym list and glossary at the end of this chapter for quick definitions and clear explanations of the commonly used terms and acronyms.

Myth #4: My family makes too much money (or I make too much money), so I shouldn't bother to apply for financial aid.
Fact: The formula used to calculate financial aid eligibility is complex and takes more into account than just your or your family's income. Also, some forms of financial aid—such as a PLUS Loan or an unsubsidized Stafford Loan—are available regardless of calculated financial need. The only way to be certain NOT to get financial aid is to not apply; don't shortchange yourself by not applying, even if you think you won't be eligible.

TYPES OF FINANCIAL AID

There are three categories of financial aid:

1. Grants and scholarships—aid that you don't have to pay back
2. Work-Study—aid that you earn by working
3. Loans—aid that you have to pay back

Each of these types of financial aid will be examined in greater detail, so you will be able to determine which one(s) to apply for and when and how to apply. Note that grants and scholarships are available on four levels: federal, state, school, and private.

Grants

Grants are normally awarded based on financial need. Even if you believe you won't be eligible based on your own or your family's income, don't skip this section. There are some grants awarded for academic performance and other criteria. The two most common grants, the Pell Grant and the Federal Supplemental Educational Opportunity Grant (FSEOG), are both offered by the federal government.

Federal Pell Grants

Federal Pell Grants are based on financial need and are awarded only to undergraduate students who have not yet earned a bachelor's or professional degree. For many students, Pell Grants provide a foundation of financial aid to which other aid may be added. For the year 2001–2002, the maximum award was $3,750.00. You can receive only one Pell Grant in an award year, and you may not receive Pell Grant funds for more than one school at a time.

How much you get will depend not only on your Expected Family Contribution (EFC) but also on your cost of attendance, whether you're a full-time or part-time student, and whether you attend school for a full academic year or less. You can qualify for a Pell Grant even if you are only enrolled part time in a training program. You should also be aware that some private and school-based sources of financial aid will not consider your eligibility if you haven't first applied for a Pell Grant.

Federal Supplemental Educational Opportunity Grants (FSEOG)

Priority consideration for FSEOG funds is given to students receiving Pell Grants because the FSEOG program is based on exceptional financial need. An FSEOG is similar to a Pell Grant in that it doesn't need to be paid back.

If you are eligible, you can receive between $100 and $4,000 a year in FSEOG funds depending on when you apply, your level of need, and the funding level of the school you're attending. The FSEOG differs from the Pell Grant in that it is not guaranteed that every needy student will receive one because each school is only allocated a certain amount of FSEOG funds by the federal government to distribute among all eligible students. To have the best chances of getting this grant, apply for financial aid as early as you can after January 1 of the year in which you plan to attend school.

State Grants

State grants are generally specific to the state in which you or your parents reside. If you and your parents live in the state in which you will attend school, you've got only one place to check. However, if you will attend school in another state, or your parents live in another state, be sure to check your eligibility with your state grant agency. Not all states allow their grant money to be used at out-of-state schools.

Scholarships

Scholarships are often awarded for academic merit or for special character-istics (for example, ethnic heritage, personal interests, sports, parents' career, college major, geographic location) rather than financial need. As with grants, you do not pay your award money back. Scholarships may be offered from federal, state, school, and private sources.

The best way to find scholarship money is to use one of the free search tools available on the Internet. After entering the appropriate information about yourself, a search takes place which ends with a list of those prizes for which you are eligible. Try www.fastasp.org, which bills itself as the world's largest and oldest private sector scholarship database. A couple of other good sites for conducting searches are www.college-scholarships.com and www.gripvision.com. If you don't have easy access to the Internet, or want to expand your search, your high school guidance counselors or college finan-cial aid officers also have plenty of information about available scholarship money. Also, check out your local library.

To find private sources of aid, spend a few hours in the library looking at scholarship and fellowship books or consider a reasonably priced (under $30) scholarship search service. See the Resources section at the end of this chap-ter to find contact information for search services and scholarship book titles. Also, contact some or all of the professional associations for the program you're interested in attending; some offer scholarships, while others offer information about where to find scholarships. If you're currently employed, find out if your employer has scholarship funds available. If you're a dependent student, ask your parents and other relatives to check with groups or organizations they belong to as well as their employers to see if they have scholarship programs or contests. Investigate these popular sources of scholarship money:

▶ religious organizations
▶ fraternal organizations
▶ clubs (such as Rotary, Kiwanis, American Legion, Grange, or 4-H)
▶ athletic clubs
▶ veterans' groups (such as Veterans of Foreign Wars)
▶ ethnic group associations
▶ labor unions

If you already know which school you will attend, check with a financial aid administrator (FAA) in the financial aid office to find out if you qualify for any school-based scholarships or other aid. Many schools offer merit-based aid for students with a high school GPA of a certain level or with a certain level of SAT scores in order to attract more students to their school. Check with your program's academic department to see if they maintain a bulletin board or other method of posting available scholarships.

While you are looking for sources of scholarships, continue to enhance your chances of winning one by participating in extracurricular events and volunteer activities. You should also obtain references from people who know you well and are leaders in the community, so you can submit their names and/or letters with your scholarship applications. Make a list of any awards you've received in the past or other honors that you could list on your scholarship application.

Work-Study Programs

When applying to a college or university, you can indicate that you are interested in a work-study program. Their student employment office will have the most information about how to earn money while getting your education. Work options include the following:

▶ on- or off-campus
▶ part-time or almost full-time
▶ school- or nationally based
▶ in some cases, in your major (to gain experience) or not (just to pay the bills)
▶ for money to repay student loans or to go directly toward educational expenses

If you're interested in school-based employment, the student employment office can give you details about the types of jobs offered (which can range from giving tours of the campus to prospective students to working in the cafeteria to helping other students in a student service office) and how much they pay.

You should also investigate the Federal Work-Study (FWS) program, which can be applied for on the Free Application for Federal Student Aid (FAFSA). The FWS program provides jobs for undergraduate and graduate students with financial need, allowing them to earn money to help pay education expenses. It encourages community service work and provides hands-on experience related to your course of study, when available. The amount of the FWS award depends on:

▶ when you apply (apply early!)
▶ your level of need
▶ the FWS funds available at your particular school

FWS salaries are the current federal minimum wage or higher, depending on the type of work and skills required. As an undergraduate, you will be paid by the hour (a graduate student may receive a salary), and you will receive the money directly from your school; you cannot be paid by commission or fee. The awards are not transferable from year to year, and not all schools have work-study programs in every area of study.

An advantage of working under the FWS program is that your earnings are exempt from FICA taxes if you are enrolled full-time and are working less than half-time. You will be assigned a job on-campus, in a private nonprofit organization, or a public agency that offers a public service. You may provide a community service relating to fire or other emergency service if your school

Hope Scholarship Credit

Eligible taxpayers may claim a federal income tax credit for tuition and fees up to a maximum of $1,500.00 per student (the amount is scheduled to be reindexed for inflation after 2002). The credit applies only to the first two years of postsecondary education, and students must be enrolled at least half-time in a program leading to a degree or a certificate. To find out more about the Hope Scholarship credit, log onto www.sfas.com.

Lifetime Learning Credit

Eligible taxpayers may claim a federal income tax credit for tuition and fees up to a maximum of $1,000 per student through the year 2002. After the year 2002, eligible taxpayers may claim a credit for tuition and fees up to a maximum of $2,000 per student (unlike the Hope Scholarship Credit, this amount will not be reindexed for inflation after 2002). The Lifetime Learning Credit is not limited to the first two years of postsecondary education; students in any year can be eligible, and there is no minimum enrollment requirement. For more information about the Lifetime Learning Credit, log onto www.sfas.com.

The National Merit Scholarship Corporation

This program offers about 5,000 students scholarship money each year based solely on academic performance in high school. If you are a high school senior with excellent grades and high scores on tests such as the ACT or SAT, ask your guidance counselor for details about this scholarship.

You may also be eligible to receive a scholarship from your state or school. Check with the higher education department of the relevant state or the financial aid office of the school you will attend.

has such a program. Some schools have agreements with private, for-profit companies if the work demands your fire or other emergency skills. The total wages you earn in each year cannot exceed your total FWS award for that year and you cannot work more than twenty hours per week. Your financial aid administrator (FAA) or the direct employer must consider your class schedule and your academic progress before assigning your job.

For more information about National Work Study programs, visit the Corporation for National Service website (www.cns.gov) and/or contact:

▶ National Civilian Community Corps (NCCC)—This AmeriCorps program is an 11-month residential national service program intended for 18–24-year-olds. Participants receive $4,725.00 for college tuition or to help repay education loan debt. Contact: National Civilian Community Corps, 1100 Vermont Avenue NW, Washington, DC 20525, 800-94-ACORPS.

▶ Volunteers in Service to America (VISTA)—VISTA is a part of ACTION, the deferral domestic volunteer agency. This program offers numerous benefits to college graduates with outstanding student loans. Contact: VISTA, Washington, DC 20525, Tel: 800-424-8867.

Student Loans

Although scholarships, grants, and work-study programs can help to offset the costs of higher education, they usually don't give you enough money to entirely pay your way. Most students who can't afford to pay for their entire education rely at least in part on student loans. The largest single source of these loans—and for all money for students—is the federal government. However, you can also find loan money from your state, school, and/or private sources.

Try these sites for information about the United States government's programs:

www.fedmoney.org

This site explains everything from the application process (you can actually download the applications you will need), eligibility requirements, and the different types of loans available.

www.finaid.org

Here, you can find a calculator for figuring out how much money your education will cost (and how much you will need to borrow), get instructions for filling out the necessary forms, and even information on the various types of military aid.

www.ed.gov/offices/OSFAP/students

This is the Federal Student Financial Aid Homepage. The FAFSA (Free Application for Federal Student Aid) can be filled out and submitted online. You can find a sample FAFSA in Appendix C, to help familiarize yourself with its format.

www.students.gov

This bills itself as the "student gateway to the U.S. government" and is run as a cooperative effort under the leadership of the Department of Education. You can find information about financial aid, community service, military service, career development, and much more.

You can also get excellent detailed information about different federal sources of education funding by sending away for a copy of the U.S. Department of Education's publication, *The Student Guide*. Write to: Federal Student Aid Information Center, P.O. Box 84, Washington, DC 20044, or call 800-4FED-AID.

Scholarships and Grants Just for Early Childhood Educators

Fifteen states now participate in the T.E.A.C.H. Early Childhood Project, which offers, among other benefits, scholarships for students currently working with young children in those states. For more information, visit the T.E.A.C.H. website at www.childcareservices.org/TEACH/T.E.A.C.H.%20Project.htm. You may also find scholarship opportunities through the National Association for the Education of Young Children (www.naeyc.org) or the Child Care Services Organization, a division of the United Way (http://national.unitedway.org).

Phi Delta Kappa, an international association of professional educators, also offers scholarships and grants for prospective teachers and student teaching awards. For more information, visit www.pdkintl.org.

If you make a commitment to teach in an economically or geographically needy area, you may be able to get funding from that state or local government or from an organization interested in improving education in that area. Similarly, you may get funding if you commit to teaching special education, children with disabilities, orphans, or children who are not proficient in English.

Listed below are some of the most popular federal loan programs:

Federal Perkins Loans

A Perkins Loan has the lowest interest (currently, it's 5%) of any loan available for both undergraduate and graduate students, and is offered to students with exceptional financial need. You repay your school, which lends the money to you with government funds.

Depending on when you apply, your level of need, and the funding level of the school, you can borrow up to $4,000 for each year of undergraduate study. The total amount you can borrow as an undergraduate is $20,000 if you have completed two years of undergraduate study; otherwise, you can borrow a maximum of $8,000.

The school pays you directly by check or credits your tuition account. You have nine months after you graduate (provided you were continuously enrolled at least half-time) to begin repayment, with up to ten years to pay off the entire loan.

PLUS Loans (Parent Loan for Undergraduate Students)

PLUS Loans enable parents with good credit histories to borrow money to pay the education expenses of a child who is a dependent undergraduate student enrolled at least half-time. Your parents must submit the completed forms to your school.

To be eligible, your parents will be required to pass a credit check. If they don't pass, they might still be able to receive a loan if they can show that extenuating circumstances exist or if someone who is able to pass the credit check agrees to co-sign the loan. Your parents must also meet citizenship requirements and not be in default on federal student loans of their own.

The yearly limit on a PLUS Loan is equal to your cost of attendance minus any other financial aid you receive. For instance, if your cost of attendance is $10,000 and you receive $5,000 in other financial aid, your parents could borrow up to, but no more than, $5,000. The interest rate varies, but is not to exceed 9% over the life of the loan. Your parents must begin repayment while you're still in school. There is no grace period.

Federal Stafford Loans

Stafford Loans are low-interest loans that are given to students who attend school at least half-time. The lender is the U.S. Department of Education for schools that participate in the Direct Lending program and a bank or credit union for schools that do not participate in the Direct Lending program. Stafford Loans fall into one of two categories:

Subsidized loans are awarded on the basis of financial need. You will not be charged any interest before you begin repayment or during authorized periods of deferment. The federal government subsidizes the interest during these periods.

Unsubsidized loans are not awarded on the basis of financial need. You will be charged interest from the time the loan is disbursed until it is paid in full. If you allow the interest to accumulate, it will be capitalized—that is, the interest will be added to the principal amount of your loan, and additional interest will be based upon the higher amount. This will increase the amount you have to repay.

There are many borrowing limit categories to these loans, depending on whether you get an unsubsidized or subsidized loan, which year in school you're enrolled, how long your program of study is, and if you're independent or dependent. You can have both kinds of Stafford Loans at the same time, but the total amount of money loaned at any given time cannot exceed $23,000 for a dependent undergraduate student and $46,000 as an independent undergraduate student (of which not more than $23,000 can be in subsidized Stafford Loans). The interest rate varies, but will never exceed 8.25%. An origination fee for a Stafford Loan is approximately 3% or 4% of the loan, and the fee will be deducted from each loan disbursement you receive. There is a six-month grace period after graduation before you must start repaying the loan.

State Loans

Loan money is also available from state governments. Remember that you may be able to qualify for a state loan based on your residency, your parents' residency, or the location of the school you're attending.

Alternative Loans

Alternative loans are loans either you, you and a co-borrower, or your parent can take out based on credit; usually the maximum you can borrow is for the cost of education minus all other financial aid received. Interest rates vary but are generally linked to the prime rate. Some of the many lenders who offer these types of loans are listed in the resources section at the end of this chapter. You can also ask your local bank for help or search the Internet for "alternative loans for students."

Questions to Ask Before You Take Out a Loan

In order to get the facts regarding the loan you're about to take out, ask the following questions:

1. What is the interest rate and how often is the interest capitalized? Your college's financial aid administrator (FAA) will be able to tell you this.

2. What fees will be charged? Government loans generally have an origination fee that goes to the federal government to help offset its costs, and a guarantee fee, which goes to a guaranty agency for insuring the loan. Both are deducted from the amount given to you.

3. Will I have to make any payments while still in school? It depends on the type of loan, but often you won't; depending on the type of loan, the government may even pay the interest for you while you're in school.

4. What is the grace period—the period after my schooling ends—during which no payment is required? Is the grace period long enough, realistically, for you to find a job and get on your feet? (A six-month grace period is common.)

5. When will my first payment be due and approximately how much will it be? You can get a good preview of the repayment process from the answer to this question.

6. Who exactly will hold my loan? To whom will I be sending payments? Who should I contact with questions or inform of changes in my situation? Your loan may be sold by the original lender to a secondary market institution, in which case you will be notified as to the contact information for your new lender.

7. Will I have the right to prepay the loan, without penalty, at any time? Some loan programs allow prepayment with no penalty but others do not.

8. Will deferments and forbearances be possible if I am temporarily unable to make payments? You need to find out how to apply for a deferment or forbearance if you need it.

9. Will the loan be canceled ("forgiven") if I become totally and permanently disabled, or if I die? This is always a good option to have on any loan you take out.

APPLYING FOR FINANCIAL AID

Now that you're aware of the types and sources of aid available, you will want to begin applying as soon as possible. You've heard about the Free Application for Federal Student Aid (FAFSA) many times in this chapter already, and should now have an idea of its importance. This is the form used by federal and state governments, as well as schools and private funding sources, to determine your eligibility for grants, scholarships, and loans. The easiest way to get a copy is to log onto www.ed.gov/offices/OSFAP/students, where you can find help in completing the FAFSA, and then submit the form electronically when you are finished. You can also get a copy by calling 1-800-4-FED-AID, or by stopping by your public library or your school's financial aid office. Be sure to get an original form, because photocopies of federal forms are not accepted.

The second step of the process is to create a financial aid calendar. Using any standard calendar, write in all of the application deadlines for each step of the financial aid process. This way, all vital information will be in one location, so you can see at a glance what needs to be done and when it's due. Start this calendar by writing in the date you requested your FAFSA. Then, mark down when you received it and when you sent in the completed form (or just the date you filled the form out online if you chose to complete the FAFSA electronically). Add important dates and deadlines for any other applications you need to complete for school-based or private aid as you progress though the financial aid process. Using and maintaining a calendar will help the whole financial aid process run more smoothly and give you peace of mind that the important dates are not forgotten.

When to Apply

Apply for financial aid as soon as possible after January 1 of the year in which you want to enroll in school. For example, if you want to begin school in the fall of 2003, then you should apply for financial aid as soon as possible after January 1, 2003. It is easier to complete the FAFSA after you have completed your tax return, so you may want to consider filing your taxes as early as possible as well. Do not sign, date, or send your application before January 1 of the year for which you are seeking aid. If you apply by mail, send your completed application in the envelope that came with the original application. The envelope is already addressed, and using it will make sure your application reaches the correct address.

Many students lose out on thousands of dollars in grants and loans because they file too late. Don't be one of them. Pay close attention to dates and deadlines.

After you mail in your completed FAFSA, your application will be processed in approximately four weeks. (If you file electronically, this time estimate is considerably shorter.) Then, you will receive a Student Aid Report (SAR) in the mail. The SAR will disclose your Expected Family Contribution (EFC), the number used to determine your eligibility for federal student aid. Each school you list on the application may also receive your application information if the school is set up to receive it electronically.

You must reapply for financial aid every year. However, after your first year, you will receive a Student Aid Report (SAR) in the mail before the application deadline. If no corrections need to be made, you can just sign it and send it in.

Getting Your Forms Filed

Follow these three simple steps if you are not completing and submitting the FAFSA online:

1. Get an original Federal Application for Federal Student Aid (FAFSA). Remember to pick up an original copy of this form, as photocopies are not accepted.

2. Fill out the entire FAFSA as completely as possible. Make an appointment with a financial aid counselor if you need help. Read the forms completely, and don't skip any relevant portions or forget to sign the form (or to have your parents sign the form, if required).

3. Return the FAFSA long before the deadline date. Financial aid counselors warn that many students don't file the forms before the deadline and lose out on available aid. Don't be one of those students!

Financial Need

Financial aid from many of the programs discussed in this chapter is awarded on the basis of need (the exceptions include unsubsidized Stafford, PLUS, consolidation loans, and some scholarships and grants). When you apply for federal student aid by completing the FAFSA, the information you report is used in a formula established by the United States Congress. The formula determines your Expected Family Contribution (EFC), an amount you and your family are expected to contribute toward your education. If your EFC is below a certain amount, you will be eligible for a Pell Grant, assuming you meet all other eligibility requirements.

There is no maximum EFC that defines eligibility for the other financial aid options. Instead, your EFC is used in an equation to determine your financial needs. Eligibility is a very complicated matter, but it can be simplified to the following equation: your contribution + your parents' contribution = expected family contribution (EFC). Student expense budget/cost of attendance (COA) minus EFC = your financial need.

The need analysis service or federal processor looks at the following if you are a dependent student:

▶ Family assets, including savings, stocks and bonds, real estate investments, business/farm ownership, and trusts
▶ Parents' ages and need for retirement income
▶ Number of children and other dependents in the family household
▶ Number of family members in college
▶ Cost of attendance, also called student expense budget, includes tuition and fees, books and supplies, room and board (living with parents, on campus, or off campus), transportation, personal expenses, and special expenses such as childcare

A financial aid administrator calculates your cost of attendance and subtracts the amount you and your family are expected to contribute toward that cost. If there's anything left over, you're considered to have financial need.

Are You Considered Dependent or Independent?

Federal policy uses strict and specific criteria to make this designation, and that criteria applies to all applicants for federal student aid equally. A dependent student is expected to have parental contribution to school expenses; an independent student is not.

You're an independent student if at least one of the following applies to you:

► you were born before January 1, 1979 (for the 2002–2003 school year)
► you're married (even if you're separated)
► you have legal dependents other than a spouse who get more than half of their support from you and will continue to get that support during the award year
► you're an orphan or ward of the court (or were a ward of the court until age 18)
► you're a graduate or professional student
► you're a veteran of the U.S. Armed Forces—formerly engaged in active service in the U.S. Army, Navy, Air Force, Marines, or Coast Guard or as a cadet or midshipman at one of the service academies—released under a condition other than dishonorable. (ROTC students, members of the National Guard, and most reservists are not considered veterans, nor are cadets and midshipmen still enrolled in one of the military service academies.)

If you live with your parents, and if they claimed you as a dependent on their last tax return, then your need will be based on your parents' income. You do not qualify for independent status just because your parents have decided to not claim you as an exemption on their tax return (this used to be the case but is no longer) or do not want to provide financial support for your college education.

Students are classified as *dependent* or *independent* because federal student aid programs are based on the idea that students (and their parents or spouse, if applicable) have the primary responsibility for paying for their post-secondary education. If your family situation is unusually complex and you believe it affects your dependency status, speak to a financial aid counselor at the school you plan to attend as soon as possible. In extremely limited cir-cumstances a financial aid office can make a professional judgment to change a student's dependency status, but this requires a great deal of documentation from the student and is not done on a regular basis. The financial aid office's decision on dependency status is *final* and cannot be appealed to the U.S. Department of Education.

Gathering Financial Records

Your financial need for most grants and loans depends on your financial sit-uation. Now that you've determined if you are considered a dependent or independent student, you will know whose financial records you need to gather for this step of the process. If you are a dependent student, then you must gather not only your own financial records, but also those of your par-ents because you must report their income and assets as well as your own when you complete the FAFSA. If you are an independent student, then you need to gather only your own financial records (and those of your spouse if you're married). Gather your tax records from the year prior to the one in

Filling Out the FAFSA

To help you fill out the FAFSA, gather the following documents:

- United States Income Tax Returns (IRS Form 1040, 1040A, or 1040EZ) for the year that just ended and W-2 and 1099 forms
- records of untaxed income, such as Social Security benefits, AFDC or ADC, child support, welfare, pensions, military subsistence allowances, and veterans' benefits
- current bank statements and mortgage information
- medical and dental expenses for the past year that weren't covered by health insurance
- business and/or farm records
- records of investments such as stocks, bonds, and mutual funds, as well as bank Certificates of Deposit (CDs) and recent statements from money market accounts
- Social Security number(s)

which you are applying. For example, if you apply for the fall of 2003, you will use your tax records from 2002.

Even if you do not complete your federal income tax return until March or April, you should not wait to file your FAFSA until your tax returns are filed with the IRS. Instead, use estimated income information and submit the FAFSA, as noted earlier, just as soon as possible after January 1. Be as accurate as possible, knowing that you can correct estimates later.

Maximizing Your Eligibility for Loans and Scholarships

Loans and scholarships are often awarded based on an individual's eligibility. Depending on the type of loan or scholarship you pursue, the eligibility requirements will be different. EStudentLoan.com (www.estudentloan.com/workshop.asp) offers the following tips and strategies for improving your eligibility when applying for loans and/or scholarships:

1. Save money in the parent's name, not the student's name.
2. Pay off consumer debt, such as credit card and auto loan balances.
3. Parents considering going back to school should do so at the same time as their children. Often, the more family members in school simultaneously, the more aid will be available to each.
4. Spend student assets and income first, before other assets and income.
5. If you believe that your family's financial circumstances are unusual, make an appointment with the financial aid administrator at your school to review your case. Sometimes the school will be able to adjust your financial aid package to compensate.
6. Minimize capital gains.
7. Do not withdraw money from your retirement fund to pay for school. If you must use this money, borrow from your retirement fund.
8. Minimize educational debt.
9. Ask grandparents to wait until the grandchild graduates before giving them money to help with their education.
10. Trust funds are generally ineffective at sheltering money from the need analysis process, and can backfire on you.

11. If you have a second home, and you need a home equity loan, take the equity loan on the second home and pay off the mortgage on the primary home.

GENERAL GUIDELINES FOR LOANS

Before you commit yourself to any loans, be sure to keep in mind that they need to be repaid. Estimate realistically how much you will earn when you leave school, remembering that you will have other monthly obligations such as housing, food, and transportation expenses.

Once You're In School

Once you have your loan (or loans) and you're attending classes, don't forget about the responsibility of your loan. Keep a file of information on your loan that includes copies of all your loan documents and related correspondence, along with a record of all your payments. Open and read all your mail about your education loan(s).

Remember also that you are obligated by law to notify both your financial aid administrator (FAA) and the holder or servicer of your loan if there is a change in your:

▶ name
▶ address
▶ enrollment status (dropping to less than half-time means that you will have to begin payment six months later)
▶ anticipated graduation date

After You Leave School

After graduation, you must begin repaying your student loan immediately, or begin after a grace period. For example, if you have a Stafford Loan you will be provided with a six-month grace period before your first payment is due;

other types of loans have grace periods as well. If you haven't been out in the working world before, your loan repayment begins your credit history. If you make payments on time, you will build up a good credit rating, and credit will be easier for you to obtain for other things. Get off to a good start, so you don't run the risk of going into default. If you default (or refuse to pay back your loan) any number of the following things could happen to you as a result. You may:

▶ have trouble getting any kind of credit in the future.
▶ no longer qualify for federal or state educational financial aid.
▶ have holds placed on your college records.
▶ have your wages garnished.
▶ have future federal income tax refunds taken.
▶ have your assets seized.

To avoid the negative consequences of going into default in your loan, be sure to do the following:

▶ Open and read all mail you receive about your education loans immediately.
▶ Make scheduled payments on time; since interest is calculated daily, delays can be costly.
▶ Contact your servicer immediately if you can't make payments on time; he or she may be able to get you into a graduated or income-sensitive/income contingent repayment plan or work with you to arrange a deferment or forbearance.

There are a few circumstances under which you won't have to repay your loan. If you become permanently and totally disabled, you probably will not have to (providing the disability did not exist prior to your obtaining the aid) repay your loan. Likewise, if you die, if your school closes permanently in the middle of the term, or if you are erroneously certified for aid by the financial aid office you will probably also not have to repay your loan. However, if you're simply disappointed in your program of study or don't get the job you wanted after graduation, you are not relieved of your obligation.

Loan Repayment

When it comes time to repay your loan, you will make payments to your original lender, to a secondary market institution to which your lender has sold your loan, or to a loan servicing specialist acting as its agent to collect payments. At the beginning of the process, try to choose the lender who offers you the best benefits (for example, a lender who lets you pay electronically, offers lower interest rates to those who consistently pay on time, or who has a toll-free number to call 24 hours a day, 7 days a week). Ask the financial aid administrator at your college to direct you to such lenders.

Be sure to check out your repayment options before borrowing. Lenders are required to offer repayment plans that will make it easier to pay back your loans. Your repayment options may include:

- ▶ *Standard repayment*: full principal and interest payments due each month throughout your loan term. You will pay the least amount of interest using the standard repayment plan, but your monthly payments may seem high when you're just out of school.
- ▶ *Graduated repayment*: interest-only or partial interest monthly payments due early in repayment. Payment amounts increase thereafter. Some lenders offer interest-only or partial interest repayment options, which provide the lowest initial monthly payments available.
- ▶ *Income-based repayment*: monthly payments are based on a percentage of your monthly income.
- ▶ *Consolidation loan*: allows the borrower to consolidate several types of federal student loans with various repayment schedules into one loan. This loan is designed to help student or parent borrowers simplify their loan repayments. The interest rate on a consolidation loan may be lower than what you're currently paying on one or more of your loans. The phone number for loan consolidation at the William D. Ford Direct Loan Program is 800-557-7392. Financial aid administrators recommend that you do not consolidate a Perkins Loan with any other loans since the interest on a Perkins Loan is already the lowest available. Loan consolidation is not available from all lenders.
- ▶ *Prepayment*: paying more than is required on your loan each month or in a lump sum is allowed for all federally sponsored loans at any time

during the life of the loan without penalty. Prepayment will reduce the total cost of your loan.

It's quite possible—in fact likely—that while you're still in school your FFELP (Federal Family Education Loan Program) loan will be sold to a secondary market institution such as Sallie Mae. You will be notified of the sale by letter, and you need not worry if this happens—your loan terms and conditions will remain exactly the same or they may even improve. Indeed, the sale may give you repayment options and benefits that you would not have had otherwise. Your payments after you finish school, and your requests for information should be directed to the new loan holder.

If you receive any interest-bearing student loans, you will have to attend exit counseling after graduation, where the loan lenders or financial aid office personnel will tell you the total amount of debt and work out a payment schedule with you to determine the amount and dates of repayment. Many loans do not become due until at least six to nine months after you graduate, giving you a grace period. For example, you do not have to begin paying on the Perkins Loan until nine months after you graduate. This grace period is to give you time to find a good job and start earning money. However, during this time, you may have to pay the interest on your loan.

If for some reason you remain unemployed when your payments become due, you may receive an unemployment deferment for a certain length of time. For many loans, you will have a maximum repayment period of ten years (excluding periods of deferment and forbearance).

THE MOST FREQUENTLY ASKED QUESTIONS ABOUT FINANCIAL AID

Here are answers to some of the most frequently asked questions about student financial aid:

1. *I probably don't qualify for aid—should I apply for it anyway?*
   Yes. Many students and families mistakenly think they don't qualify for aid and fail to apply. Remember that there are some sources of aid that are not based on need. The FAFSA form is free—there's no good reason for not applying.

2. *Do I have to be a U.S. citizen to qualify for financial aid?*
   Students (and parents, for PLUS Loans) must be U.S. citizens or eligible noncitizens to receive federal and state financial aid. Eligible noncitizens are U.S. nationals or U.S. permanent nonresidents (with "green cards"), as well as nonresidents in certain special categories. If you don't know whether you qualify, speak to a financial aid counselor as soon as possible.

3. *Do I have to register with the Selective Service before I can receive financial aid?*
   Male students who are U.S. citizens or eligible noncitizens must register with the Selective Service by the appropriate deadline in order to receive federal financial aid. Call the Selective Service at 847-688-6888 if you have questions about registration.

4. *Do I need to be admitted at a particular university before I can apply for financial aid?*
   No. You can apply for financial aid any time after January 1. However, to get the funds, you must be admitted and enrolled in school.

5. *Do I have to reapply for financial aid every year?*
   Yes, and if your financial circumstances change, you may get either more or less aid. After your first year you will receive a Renewal Application which contains preprinted information from the previous year's FAFSA. Renewal of your aid also depends on your making satisfactory progress toward a degree and achieving a minimum GPA.

6. *Are my parents responsible for my educational loans?*
   No. You and you alone are responsible, unless they endorse or co-sign your loan. Parents are, however, responsible for federal PLUS Loans. If your parents (or grandparents or uncle or distant cousins) want to help pay off your loan, you can have your billing statements sent to their address.

7. *If I take a leave of absence from school, do I have to start repaying my loans?*
   Not immediately, but you will after the grace period. Generally, though, if you use your grace period up during your leave, you will have to begin repayment immediately after graduation, unless you apply for an extension of the grace period before it's used up.

8. *If I get assistance from another source, should I report it to the student financial aid office?*

Yes—and, unfortunately, your aid amount will possibly be lowered accordingly. But you will get into trouble later on if you don't report it.

9. *Are federal work-study earnings taxable?*

Yes, you must pay federal and state income tax, although you may be exempt from FICA taxes if you are enrolled full time and work less than 20 hours a week.

10. *My parents are separated or divorced. Which parent is responsible for filling out the FAFSA?*

If your parents are separated or divorced, the custodial parent is responsible for filling out the FAFSA. The custodial parent is the parent with whom you lived the most during the past 12 months. Note that this is not necessarily the same as the parent who has legal custody. The question of which parent must fill out the FAFSA becomes complicated in many situations, so you should take your particular circumstance to the student financial aid office for help.

Financial Aid Checklist

____ Explore your options as soon as possible once you've decided to begin a training program.

____ Find out what your school requires and what financial aid they offer.

____ Complete and mail the FAFSA as soon as possible after January 1.

____ Complete and mail other applications by the deadlines.

____ Return all requested documentation promptly to your financial aid office.

____ Carefully read all letters and notices from the school, the federal student aid processor, the need analysis service, and private scholarship organizations. Note whether financial aid will be sent before or after you are notified about admission, and how exactly you will receive the money.

____ Gather loan application information and forms from your school or college financial aid office. You must forward the completed loan application to your financial aid office for processing. Don't forget to sign the loan application.

____ Report any changes in your financial resources or expenses to your financial aid office so they can adjust your award accordingly.

____ Re-apply each year.

Financial Aid Acronyms Key

COA	Cost of Attendance (also known as COE, Cost of Education)
CWS	College Work-Study
EFC	Expected Family Contribution
EFT	Electronic Funds Transfer
ESAR	Electronic Student Aid Report
ETS	Educational Testing Service
FAA	Financial Aid Administrator
FAF	Financial Aid Form
FAFSA	Free Application for Federal Student Aid
FAO	Financial Aid Office/Financial Aid Officer
FDSLP	Federal Direct Student Loan Program
FFELP	Federal Family Education Loan Program
FSEOG	Federal Supplemental Educational Opportunity Grant
FWS	Federal Work-Study
PC	Parent Contribution
PLUS	Parent Loan for Undergraduate Students
SAP	Satisfactory Academic Progress
SC	Student Contribution
USED	U.S. Department of Education

FINANCIAL AID TERMS—CLEARLY DEFINED

accrued interest—interest that accumulates on the unpaid principal balance of your loan

capitalization of interest—addition of accrued interest to the principal balance of your loan that increases both your total debt and monthly payments

default—failure to repay your education loan

deferment—a period when a borrower, who meets certain criteria, may suspend loan payments

delinquency—failure to make payments when due

disbursement—loan funds issued by the lender

forbearance—temporary adjustment to repayment schedule for cases of financial hardship

grace period—specified period of time after you graduate or leave school during which you need not make payments

holder—the institution that currently owns your loan

in-school grace, and **deferment interest subsidy**—interest the federal government pays for borrowers on some loans while the borrower is in school, during authorized deferments, and during grace periods

interest-only payment—a payment that covers only interest owed on the loan and none of the principal balance

interest—cost you pay to borrow money

lender (originator)—puts up the money when you take out a loan; most lenders are financial institutions, but some state agencies and schools make loans too

origination fee—fee, deducted from the principal, which is paid to the federal government to offset its cost of the subsidy to borrowers under certain loan programs

principal—amount you borrow, which may increase as a result of capitalization of interest, and the amount on which you pay interest

promissory note—contract between you and the lender that includes all the terms and conditions under which you promise to repay your loan

secondary markets—institutions that buy student loans from originating lenders, thus providing lenders with funds to make new loans

servicer—organization that administers and collects your loan; may be either the holder of your loan or an agent acting on behalf of the holder

subsidized Stafford Loans—loans based on financial need; the government pays the interest on a subsidized Stafford Loan for borrowers while they are in school and during specified deferment periods

unsubsidized Stafford Loans—loans available to borrowers, regardless of family income; unsubsidized Stafford Loan borrowers are responsible for the interest during in-school, deferment periods, and repayment

FINANCIAL AID RESOURCES

In addition to the sources listed throughout this chapter, these are additional resources that may be used to obtain more information about financial aid.

Telephone Numbers

Federal Student Aid Information Center (U. S. Department of Education)

Hotline	800-4FED-AID
	(800-433-3243)
TDD Number for Hearing-Impaired	800-730-8913
For suspicion of fraud or abuse of federal aid	800-MIS-USED
	(800-647-8733)
Selective Service	847-688-6888
Immigration and Naturalization (INS)	415-705-4205
Internal Revenue Service (IRS)	800-829-1040
Social Security Administration	800-772-1213
National Merit Scholarship Corporation	708-866-5100
Sallie Mae's college AnswerSM Service	800-222-7183
Career College Association	202-336-6828
ACT: American College Testing program	916-361-0656
(about forms submitted to the	
need analysis servicer)	
College Scholarship Service (CSS)	609-771-7725;
	TDD 609-883-7051
Need Access/Need Analysis Service	800-282-1550
FAFSA on the Web Processing/	800-801-0576
Software Problems	

Websites

www.ed.gov/prog_info/SFAStudentGuide

The Student Guide is a free informative brochure about financial aid and is available on-line at the Department of Education's Web address listed here.

www.ed.gov\prog_info\SFA\FAFSA

This site offers students help in completing the FAFSA.

www.ed.gov/offices/OPE/t4_codes

This site offers a list of Title IV school codes that you may need to complete the FAFSA.

www.ed.gov/offices/OPE/express

This site enables you to fill out and submit the FAFSA on line. You will need to print out, sign, and send in the release and signature pages.

www.career.org

This is the website of the Career College Association (CCA). It offers a limited number of scholarships for attendance at private proprietary schools. You can also contact CCA at 750 First Street, NE, Suite 900, Washington, DC 20002-4242.

www.salliemae.com

This is the website for Sallie Mae that contains information about loan programs.

www.teri.org

This is the website of The Educational Resource Institute (TERI), which offers alternative loans to students and parents.

www.nelliemae.com

This is the website for Nellie Mae; it contains information about alternative loans as well as federal loans for students and parents.

www.key.com

This is Key Bank's website, which has information on alternative loans for parents and students.

www.educaid.com

This is the website for Educaid, which offers both federal and alternative loans to students and parents.

Software Programs

Cash for Class

Tel: 800-205-9581

Fax: 714-673-9039

Redheads Software, Inc.

3334 East Coast Highway #216

Corona del Mar, CA 92625

E-mail: cashclass@aol.com

C-LECT Financial Aid Module

Chronicle Guidance Publications

P.O. Box 1190

Moravia, NY 13118-1190

Tel: 800-622-7284 or 315-497-0330

Fax: 315-497-3359

Peterson's Award Search

Peterson's

P.O. Box 2123

Princeton, NJ 08543-2123

Tel: 800-338-3282 or 609-243-9111

E-mail: custsvc@petersons.com

Pinnacle Peak Solutions

(Scholarships 101)

Pinnacle Peak Solutions

7735 East Windrose Drive

Scottsdale, AZ 85260

Tel: 800-762-7101 or 602-951-9377

Fax: 602-948-7603

TP Software—Student Financial Aid

Search Software

TP Software

P.O. Box 532

Bonita, CA 91908-0532

Tel: 800-791-7791 or 619-496-8673

E-mail: mail@tpsoftware.com

Books and Pamphlets

The Student Guide
Published by the U.S. Department of Education, this is the handbook about federal aid programs. To get a printed copy, call 1-800-4-FED-AID.

Looking for Student Aid
Published by the U.S. Department of Education, this is an overview of sources of information about financial aid. To get a printed copy, call 1-800-4-FED-AID.

How Can I Receive Financial Aid for College?
Published from the Parent Brochures ACCESS ERIC website. Order a printed copy by calling 800-LET-ERIC or write to ACCESS ERIC, Research Blvd-MS 5F, Rockville, MD 20850-3172.

Cassidy, David J. *The Scholarship Book 2002: The Complete Guide to Private-Sector Scholarships, Fellowships, Grants, and Loans for the Undergraduate.* (Englewood Cliffs, NJ: Prentice Hall, 2001).

Chany, Kalman A. and Geoff Martz. *Student Advantage Guide to Paying for College 1997 Edition.* (New York: Random House, The Princeton Review, 1997.)

College Costs & Financial Aid Handbook, 18th ed. (New York: The College Entrance Examination Board, 1998).

Cook, Melissa L. *College Student's Handbook to Financial Assistance and Planning* (Traverse City, MI: Moonbeam Publications, Inc., 1991).

Davis, Kristen. *Financing College: How to Use Savings, Financial Aid, Scholarships, and Loans to Afford the School of Your Choice* (Washington, DC: Random House, 1996).

Hern, Davis and Joyce Lain Kennedy. *College Financial Aid for Dummies* (Foster City, CA: IDG Books Worldwide, 1999).

Peterson's Scholarships, Grants and Prizes 2002 (Princeton, NJ: Peterson's, 2001).

Ragins, Marianne. *Winning Scholarships for College: An Insider's Guide* (New York: Henry Holt & Company, 1994).

Scholarships, Grants & Prizes: Guide to College Financial Aid from Private Sources. (Princeton, NJ: Peterson's, 1998).

Schwartz, John. *College Scholarships and Financial Aid* (New York: Simon & Schuster, Macmillan, 1995).

Schlacter, Gail and R. David Weber. *Scholarships 2000* (New York: Kaplan, 1999).

Other Related Financial Aid Books

Annual Register of Grant Support (Chicago, IL: Marquis, annual).
A's and B's of Academic Scholarships (Alexandria, VA: Octameron, annual).
Chronicle Student Aid Annual (Moravia, NY: Chronicle Guidance, annual).
College Blue Book. Scholarships, Fellowships, Grants and Loans (New York: Macmillan, annual).
College Financial Aid Annual (New York: Prentice Hall, annual).
Directory of Financial Aids for Minorities (San Carlos, CA: Reference Service Press, biennial).
Directory of Financial Aids for Women (San Carlos, CA: Reference Service Press, biennial).
Financial Aids for Higher Education (Dubuque, IA: Wm. C. Brown, biennial).
Financial Aid for the Disabled and their Families (San Carlos, CA: Reference Service Press, biennial).
Leider, Robert and Ann. *Don't Miss Out: the Ambitious Student's Guide to Financial Aid* (Alexandria, VA: Octameron, annual).
Paying Less for College (Princeton, NJ: Peterson's, annual).

THE INSIDE TRACK

Who: Ellen Bonham
What: Music Teacher
Where: Champaign, Illinois

INSIDER'S STORY

I have a degree in music education and have taught private piano lessons, public and private school music, and was a vocal coach and accompanist for the San Francisco Boys Chorus. I have always enjoyed working most with young children—from preschool through the second grade. I found a lack of music-training classes geared toward that age. Several other mothers I knew were looking for music classes to enroll their own small children in, so I decided to begin teaching early childhood music classes in my own home. I thought that it would be a wonderful experience and a great way to work at home while my children were small. I have a large family room with a comfy rug, a piano, and lots of room to move that is perfect for music classes. I also invested in rhythm instruments, bells, and some other instruments that the children could play and experiment with. Then, I posted ads for classes, which I called The Joy of Singing, where parents were coming and going—grocery stores, nursery schools, also on music school bulletin boards. Most of my students joined The Joy of Singing via word of mouth.

I absolutely love my job. There are so many rewards when teaching young children. They constantly surprise me, and I find myself learning as much from them as they learn from me. Music is a profession in which you can see the results of your teaching immediately. A young child's excitement and enthusiasm when a new song or music skill is presented is so exciting to watch—their whole bodies move in-time and their faces exude cheer and earnestness. When the music is presented in the right way, young learners are like sponges. Children who cannot even read or write yet, can comprehend rather sophisticated concepts, particularly regarding music and rhythm reading. They hear well and can learn to distinguish musical instruments and any number of things relating to form in music. Many ideas that they absorb in music apply to other skills and subjects they learn later, in school.

Because the kind of learning we do in music is so active and such fun, most children love coming to my classes. The attention span is, of course, very short at this age so switching activities helps keep the children moving so that they don't become too restless. I think my classes also helped the students become better listeners and socializers, not only in music, but also in other aspects of their lives; Cooperation, sharing, and listening were all values I enforced in my classes. One of the most important things that I learned on the job was to be consistent in discipline and to be clear about my expectations. Children do not always do what we want them to do; therefore learning how to use their psychologies and personalities to manage their behavior is a real challenge. Studying the way the brain works and the stages of development is very helpful to any early childhood educator. In addition, asking children directly about what works and doesn't with certain activities can really help you plan for future classes.

CHAPTER four

LANDING YOUR FIRST JOB:
WHERE AND HOW TO FIND THE RIGHT POSITION

THIS CHAPTER provides a questionnaire to help you determine what sort of job is best for you and then describes a wealth of resources to assist you in your job search. You will get the inside scoop on conducting your job search—from networking and using online career resources to attending job fairs and answering classified ads.

WHETHER YOU ARE already working in early childhood education or just getting started, once you complete your certification or degree, you will be qualified for a greater range of jobs with a greater range of schools and institutions. If you are very lucky, you may already have the ideal job waiting for you when you graduate; but if you are like most early childhood educators, you will have to spend considerable time and effort looking for the job that is right for you. Fortunately, there are many strategies and resources you can use to find your first job as a certified or degreed early childhood educator. The first step is to figure out just what kind of job is right for you.

NARROWING YOUR OPTIONS:
WHAT'S THE RIGHT JOB FOR YOU?

Even if your certification or degree limits you to working with specific age groups or types of children, you still have a wide range of choices when you begin your search for a position as an early childhood educator. Because there are so many different types of childcare and preschool arrangements, it is important to determine exactly what kind of work you should look for before you begin your job search.

Depending on your education and experience, you may be eligible to teach in many different kinds of schools and childcare situations, from large preschools to small homecare centers or individual family care. But not every setting is right for you, and you will be most comfortable with an employer who shares your educational philosophy and enables you to achieve your specific career and personal goals.

To help you determine what kind of preschool, childcare center, or other childcare arrangement will work best for you, answer the following questions carefully.

Early Childhood Educator Job Type Questionnaire

1. What are your specific early childhood education qualifications? (Include both your education and experience.)

   _____

   _____

   _____

2. For which of the following job titles are you qualified? Check all that apply.
   - nanny/au pair _____
   - teacher's aide _____
   - assistant teacher/childcare provider, infant/toddler (0–3) _____
   - assistant teacher/childcare provider, preschool (3–5) _____
   - childcare provider, infant/toddler (0–3) _____
   - childcare provider, preschool (3–5) _____
   - preschool teacher _____
   - head teacher _____
   - director _____

3. What are your specific talents and interests? List at least three below.
   Example:
   • *fluent in Spanish and French*
   • *playing piano and singing*
   • *music therapy*
   • *infant/toddler care*
   • *special education*
   • *bilingual/English as a second language education*
   • *foreign language instruction*
   • *music and arts education*
   • *technology*

   _____

   _____

   _____

4. What are your *short-term* career goals?
   Example: Find job at a school where music is a major part of the curriculum;
   develop ideas and practices for using music in a preschool setting.

   _____

   _____

5. What are your *long-term* career goals?
   Example: Return to school for certificate in curriculum development; become
   music program director for large preschool.

   _____

   _____

6. What type of early childhood care school or setting is most appealing
   to you? Rank the following in order of preference.
   • single family/residential childcare (nanny) _____
   • small group home care (family childcare provider) _____
   • small–medium sized non-affiliated childcare center/preschool ___
   • medium–large sized non-affiliated childcare center/preschool _____
   • Montessori school _____
   • corporate childcare center _____
   • religious institution childcare center/preschool _____
   • childcare center/preschool at a sports center, recreation center, or
     other institution _____

Would you prefer:

- A privately owned center or school or a public institution?
- An independent center or school or one that is part of a local or national chain (such as KinderCare Learning Centers)?
- A center or school for infants–prekindergarten only or one that also provides primary education (kindergarten and up)?

7. How far are you willing to travel to and from work? Are you willing to relocate? _____

   _____

8. How important is the size of the school or center you work for? What is your ideal child to childcare provider ratio? Your ideal total number of children in care?

   _____

   _____

9. What is your educational philosophy? Describe your main principles and beliefs in a few short sentences below.

   _____

   _____

   _____

10. Is there a specific type of child with whom you would like to work? Check all relevant boxes below.
    - special education—physical disability
    - special education—mental disability
    - special education—physical and/or mental disability
    - bilingual children
    - economically disadvantaged children
    - ethnically diverse group of children
    - other _____

    Why do you want to work with this particular group?

    _____

    _____

11. Do you want to work with children in one age group only (e.g., 1–2 year olds) or would you like to work with a range of ages (e.g., 1–4 year olds in a mixed group)?

    _____

    _____

Answering these questions will not only help you focus your job search; it will also help you prepare your cover letters and resume and perform well in interviews because you have already gathered this key information in one place. After all, when you know exactly what kind of job you are looking for, it is easier to find it—and land it.

WHERE TO LOOK FOR JOB OPENINGS

According to the U.S. Department of Labor's 2000–2001 *Occupational Outlook Handbook*, "Employment of preschool teachers and childcare workers is projected to increase faster than average for all occupations through the year 2008." Even in a tight economy, the job outlook for early childhood education is good; parents are increasingly aware of the importance of good care in a child's most formative years, and the trend toward families with two working parents remains strong. Even stay-at-home moms often enroll their children at least part time in day care or preschool so they can interact with other children, get accustomed to a learning environment, and develop critical early skills through lessons and structured play. So the job you want is out there; now it is time to find it.

The rest of this chapter describes the following job hunting resources for early childhood educators:

- ▶ schools/educational institutions
- ▶ internships/student teaching experiences
- ▶ job fairs
- ▶ networking
- ▶ newspapers and other publications
- ▶ the Internet
- ▶ childcare organizations and networks
- ▶ cold calls

Your School

One of the benefits of attending a school for an early childhood degree or certificate is that you can make use of the school's career services programs. Most schools have a career placement office, and depending upon the size and resources of your program, the education department may also have its own job placement resources as well. These resources can range from a low-tech bulletin board to a sophisticated online job bank. For example, Wheelock College's Career Planning Office posts local job listings for each of the school's major programs (teaching, early childhood education, and social services) on the school's website, and detailed job descriptions for those postings are available in the Career Planning Office. However job opportunities are handled, your educational institution can provide dozens of opportunities that can lead to a terrific position.

In addition, your school should be able to provide you with lists of job fairs and conferences that may lead to excellent networking opportunities in early childhood education.

Student Teaching/Internship Experiences

Your student teaching or internship experience may also open doors for your first full-time position. A job may open where you are student teaching, and you already have a leg up on the competition. For one thing, it is a place in which you are already comfortable—you are already familiar with the school

Being Your Own Boss

Do you dream of having your own homecare, preschool, or childcare center? Your best bet is to gain several years of experience working in a center or school similar to the kind you would like to have someday. And "be patient," advises Savitri Gulick, owner of The Children's House, a homecare provider in South Orange, New Jersey. Ms. Gulick worked for others for nearly eleven years before opening her own home care. She says she has seen many people start their own childcare only to quit after a few months. "You have to stick it out," says Gulick because there is always a learning curve when you go out on your own. Gulick also advises self-employed early childhood educators to take advantage of government and school seminars and training programs that can help you improve your business and management skills.

or center's philosophy, curriculum, culture, and most important, its students. Furthermore, you have a sizeable advantage in the hiring process because the teachers and administrators already know you and your teaching style—if you have enjoyed your student teaching job or internship, it is probably worthwhile asking about any available full-time positions once you are credentialed or certified.

Job Fairs

Job fairs—gatherings of prospective employers who sponsor information booths where prospective employees learn about employers and their available job opportunities—are another important job-hunting resource, especially for educators. There may be job fairs sponsored by your department, by your school, or by local school districts. Job fairs are a great way to network, to find out about schools and centers in your area, and get your resume in the hands of a variety of different employers. Sometimes administrators conduct interviews during the job fair, and occasionally, depending upon the urgency of the vacancy, teachers are hired on the spot, pending criminal background checks and other pre-employment verification. Check with your school and education department for a schedule of job fairs for early childhood educators.

Wanted: Teachers to Teach the Teachers

Here's a career path you may not have considered: earning a graduate degree so you can teach others how to be effective early childhood educators. According to Dr. Deborah Ceglowski, Professor of Early Childhood Education at the University of Minnesota in Minneapolis, "there are tons of opportunities for teaching early childhood education classes at the college level." Job qualifications vary, but you will be eligible to teach in most two-year programs and community colleges with a master's degree in early childhood education. Programs that award a four-year bachelor's degree usually require faculty to have an EdD or PhD.

Making Job Fairs Work for You

1. **Preregister whenever possible**. Employers often prescreen job fair attendees and will sometimes set up interviews for the day of the fair with job candidates who have preregistered. In any case, preregistering makes it possible for you to catch a prospective employer's attention early on. You may even get calls from employers you hadn't planned on visiting or didn't have the time to meet.

2. **Research the job fair participants**. Get a list of the schools and centers that will attend the job fair in advance and find out as much as you can about each participant. Then you can narrow down the list to the most desirable employers. This will make the time you spend at the fair more productive—you will be sure to visit your top choices instead of wandering around from booth to booth and possibly missing opportunities you really want. In addition, when you speak to a representative from a place you would like to work, which you know because of your background research, you will have more to talk about and will be able to ask more intelligent questions. Potential employers are really interested in job candidates who have taken the time to prepare for a meeting. All of this makes you a more memorable and more desirable candidate because it reflects on how you will conduct yourself on the job and in the classroom.

3. **Set up a game plan**. Arrive early and get a sense of the layout of the job fair before the booths get crowded. Plan your approach in advance: Know where you are going to go, in what order, and rehearse your introduction. Have a list of questions you want to ask each employer, and be prepared to answer any questions you may be asked. (Interview strategies are discussed in detail in Chapter 5.)

4. **Dress appropriately.** Present yourself as a professional by arriving dressed for a job interview. Make sure you wear a legible nametag prominently displayed on your lapel or chest area (preferably on the right-hand side, so your nametag is in the line of vision when someone is shaking your hand). And wear comfortable shoes; you will probably be on your feet for hours.

5. **Bring extra copies of your resume(s).** Be sure to have plenty of copies of your resume (or resumes) so that potential employers have a way to contact you and review your skills and accomplishments. If you have more than one resume, organize them so you give the right resume to the right person.

6. **Network.** Job fairs also provide a terrific opportunity to expand your network. Make sure you have business cards that you can distribute to everyone you meet. All you need is your name and contact information; each card you hand out can lead to a

key contact or a phone call from a prospective employer, or a job tip from another contact you have made.

Here's a sample of a business card:

Wendy Ng
Certified Infant and Toddler Care
433 Winslow Drive
Wethersfield, CT 06111
860-555-4567
wendy.ng@ng.mail.com

Take good notes that include the names and contact information of people you meet; record as much as you can about each conversation. For example, under the name and contact information for a school representative, write down the questions you were asked, if the representative seemed to be particularly impressed with one or more of your answers, and/or if you had difficulty responding to a particular question. This way when you follow up after the job fair, you can reiterate your strong points and craft a more articulate answer to any questions that may have given you difficulty.

7. **Follow up.** Within a few days of the job fair, send a follow-up letter to everyone you met. Restate your interest, your qualifications, and your desire for an interview.

Your Network

As the saying goes, it's not *what* you know, but *who* you know. For better or for worse, simply knowing the right people can often give you a tremendous advantage as you search for work. So spread the news. Tell everyone—your friends and family, your acquaintances from clubs and organizations—that you are looking for work as an early childhood educator. Ask them if they know of any positions and/or if they will pass your name along to people they know who work or have contacts in the field of early childhood education. You never know—a friend of a friend can give you a great job lead.

Be especially sure to contact those people in your network who are involved in education—the teachers and administrators you met through internships or student teaching opportunities and any previous employers if you have had prior experience in childcare. Now that you have your certificate or degree, you may be a candidate for higher-level positions that have become available in places you used to work, or with people with whom you used to work.

Remember to keep good notes about whom you talk to, when you talk to them, and the information you receive from them. You may want to refer to that information in the weeks or months ahead.

Newspapers and Other Publications

Classified ads in newspapers and job listings in publications by educational organizations are another important source of job leads. Every Sunday, for example, *The New York Times* publishes a special "Careers in Education" section. *Education Week*, the weekly newspaper of Editorial Projects in Education, Inc., offers an extensive list of education job openings each week. Your local papers (or the local papers of the area(s) in which you would like to teach) will often advertise openings in local centers or preschools. Many of these local papers can also be accessed online.

Wanted: People Who Follow Directions

When you respond to an advertisement for a job vacancy, be sure to *follow the instructions carefully*. Provide all of the documents requested in the manner in which they are requested. Don't fax if the ad asks you to call; don't call if the ad asks you to fax. And if you neglect to include one or more documents, your resume may be put on the bottom of the pile—or may never even be reviewed at all.

Online Job Hunting Resources

The Internet is an increasingly valuable resource for job hunters. Numerous general job search sites, such as the popular monster.com and hotjobs.com, are not specific to any industry or field, and they post thousands of job openings each year. These sites may be helpful, but you will probably have more success searching job banks that are designed specifically for educators, and especially those designed specifically for early childhood educators. On most of these sites, you can search job listings and post your resume, so the search goes both ways—you can find openings at various schools and centers while schools and centers also have the opportunity to find you. All of the websites below offer their job search and/or resume posting services for free, unless otherwise noted.

www.daycare.about.com/cs/jobsearch
Designed specifically for early childhood educators, this site lists job vacancies in early childhood education nationwide. Click on "America's job bank" and then "select job title." Select "education and training" and click on "preschool teacher." Then you can enter your zip code for job postings in your area. This site also provides two job banks just for nanny positions and links to job opportunities with childcare center franchises.

www.naeyc.org/profdev/default.asp
This National Association for the Education of Young Children (NAEYC) site offers job listings under the "Career Forum" section. You must be a member of the NAEYC to view current postings.

www.recruitingteachers.com
This national teacher recruitment clearinghouse contains a job bank portal that will connect you to local, state, national, and international job banks. Click on "How to Find a Job" and then on the "Job Bank" link. The site also includes tips on job hunting and provides other teacher resources.

www.teachers-teachers.com
This sophisticated site, affiliated with the American Association of Colleges for Teacher Education, allows you to create an online version of your resume and input your job search specifications, including the area(s) and type of school in which you would like to teach. When job openings meet your specified criteria, you receive an e-mail. You can review detailed infor-

mation about each job posting and click on links to those schools' websites. You can also send your cover letter via e-mail through the site.

www.cec.sped.org/cc/cc.htm

This site uses the same system as www.teachers-teachers.com, but because this version of the site is affiliated with the Council for Exceptional Children (CEC), all of the job postings are for vacancies in special education.

www.hireed.net

HireEd.net allows you to post your resume and search job postings; you can also use the search agent feature to be notified whenever there is a new job posting that matches your criteria. Anyone can post a resume, but the job search services are free only for members of the Association for Supervision and Curriculum Development (ASCD). If you are not a member of the ASCD, you can use the search agent for a small fee.

www.edweek.org/jobs.cfm

Education Week posts its "Marketplace" section here on the Web. The site lists both national and international administrative and teacher job postings and is updated weekly. You will find many of the country's top schools and organizations advertising here. The focus on this site is secondary and higher education and administrative positions, but you may find excellent opportunities.

www.careers.education.wisc.edu/ProjectConnect/MainMenu.cfm

This site, part of Project Connect: Connecting Schools and Teachers in the Information Age, offers job postings from around the country. To access the postings, you need a username and password from the institution where you received your teacher education. Check the website to find a state-by-state list of participating schools.

www.education-world.com/jobs

Once you register for the mailing list on this site, you will receive postings of jobs that match your criteria. You can also post your resume here, and the site includes links to state certification information and other teacher resources.

www.greatteacher.net

You can browse job openings and e-mail prospective employers directly from this site. The "situations wanted" section allows you to post information about yourself and your career objectives for prospective employers to browse.

www.school-jobs.net

This site allows you to post your resume and conduct a local, state or national job search. Click on "early learning" under the section "area of expertise" to begin your search. If you find an opening that interests you, you can contact the employer directly. Meanwhile, prospective employers can review your resume and contact you for an interview.

www.whohasjobs.com

On this general job search site, click on "jobs," select "education," and then select "early childhood" for listings. The site also has links for jobs in special education. Postings on this site are focused on midwestern states.

Childcare Organizations and Associations

There are numerous local and national childcare organizations and associations, such as the National Association for Family Childcare (www.nafcc.org) and the Center for the Childcare Workforce (www.ccw.org). These organizations and networks offer great opportunities for networking. You can join chat/discussion groups, attend conferences, and take advantage of other opportunities that put you in touch with other education professionals. Many of these organizations also have publications and/or websites that may include job listings. The Childcare Services Association (www.childcareservices.org), for example, a North Carolina-based United Way agency, offers numerous publications and posts early childhood job vacancies in Durham and Orange Counties. The San Francisco Early Childhood Information Project (www.sfchildnet.org) includes job listings for the area and offers numerous free seminars for early childhood educators. See Appendix A for a list of childcare organizations and associations.

Cold Calls

Finally, a great way to get your foot in the door is to express your interest in a position even if one hasn't been advertised. Who knows—maybe a vacancy will pop up in the next few weeks, or maybe there were already plans, as yet unannounced, for a new hire. If there is a school or center where you would like to work but you haven't seen or heard of any vacancies, drop off or send in your resume anyway. Let the administrators know that you are interested, and if an opening should arise, you may be the first person they will call. In your cover letter, describe what appeals to you about the school or center and why you would be a good fit for the school.

Calling All Nannies: Your Experience Counts!

One of the best ways to get valuable on-the-job experience in early childhood education is by working as a nanny for an infant or toddler. Not only can it be a great way to help finance your education, but you will also get terrific experience dealing with small children in a comfortable family atmosphere and without the pressure of dealing with a large group of children. As a nanny, you will develop your teaching personality and strategies for dealing with difficult situations, such as illness and conflicts between children, and you will get a sense of what childcare situations you are most and least comfortable in. Further, being a nanny opens the door to great networking opportunities. You are likely to meet lots of other nannies and parents who may be valuable contacts during your job search.

As you can see, once you determine what kind of job is right for you, there are many resources to help you in your search for a fulfilling position. Schools, job fairs, networking contacts, publications, the Internet, professional organizations and cold calls can all lead to excellent job opportunities. Now it's time to make sure you have a top-notch resume and successful interview.

THE INSIDE TRACK

Who: Christine Cole

What: Preschool Program Director

Where: Brooklyn, NY

INSIDER'S STORY

I am a preschool teacher at a state-funded program for low-income parents and their children. Parents qualify for the program and our services based on financial need. Many of the kids are from single-parent households, and a lot of them live with their grandparents. Several mothers drop their children off on their way to school—in community college programs and technical institutes—and it's reassuring to know that our program makes it easier for them to pursue their education.

Often, different family members take turns dropping off the children in the morning and different caretakers pick them up in the evening. I believe that the routine setting and stability that we offer at the preschool program may be the only constant that some of these children have in their lives.

My staff and I strive to help make these complicated lives more manageable, so we begin each morning with a routine mini-program to get everyone oriented and prepared for the day ahead. We serve breakfast, lunch, and an afternoon snack, so families can be sure that the children are looked after from a nutritional standpoint. Also, we have morning and afternoon quiet time, where the children may take naps as they are read to. Realistically speaking, some of these children do not get a full eight-to-ten hours of sleep each night. They are shuttled from here to the baby sitter to the home, and often they accompany their primary caregivers to the grocery store, pharmacy, and other after-work errands. They don't get a chance to settle down until the family settles in for the night, so we help them catch up on their rest during the day.

All of this is in addition to the activities that we prepare every day. We have story time, art, music, and computer lab, as well as educational game time, organized play, and counting drills. Once a week, we have an afternoon devoted to Spanish—from basic language lessons, to stories about Latin American people, places, and things, to Latin American visitors, and finally, to snack time. This week, we had mangos and guava juice for an afternoon treat!

I find my career to be rewarding and usually downright exhausting. I can't imagine doing anything else with my education, though. I feel that the my colleagues and I provide offer these children a stronghold on their future—in education and in life. They could easily fall through the cracks, but they have come here to start their school years, and that's an important choice.

My advice for students interested in early childhood education is to get involved in a good program at their school. These programs really help students prepare for employment. Because these programs are very popular and easy to find, I require coursework in early childhood education as prerequisite for employment here. I usually have no trouble finding qualified applicants. When I hire, I look for individuals who truly enjoy working with children. Other important qualities are patience, a hard-working, diligent mindset, and kindness. I look for extraverts who aren't hesitant to get down on the floor and join in the children's games when they visit the center for an interview. I seek the problem-solvers and find trustworthy partners for the program.

CHAPTER five

RESUMES, COVER LETTERS, AND ACING THE INTERVIEW

IN THIS chapter you will find the tools you need to write an effective resume and an engaging cover letter. Then, find out how to ace your interviews by practicing with commonly asked interview questions. Finally, learn how to follow up in a professional manner to get the job you want.

NOW THAT YOU are certified and you know where and how to look for a job, it's time to go out and get one. The first step to getting a job is preparing a resume and cover letter. If you write an impressive cover letter and resume and you are qualified for the job, you will land an interview. If you prepare well for the interview and follow up with a thank you letter, you will dramatically increase your chances of getting a job offer.

Don't Be Afraid to Boast a Little

Your resume has one basic purpose: to get you an interview. Your resume must convince the employer that you are a candidate worth meeting. Follow the guidelines for writing a good resume and include experiences that highlight your most valuable skills, especially those skills that are required for the job for which you are applying. For example, if you are responding to an ad for a job in early childhood education, where computer proficiency is required, include your experience in teaching senior citizens to browse the Internet. If the job ad requires excellent communication skills, list the responsibilities you had working as an announcer for the school radio station. For a job that requires experience with special education, list all those classes you took in the area and the volunteer work you did for blind children last summer. Playing up the skills and past jobs that demonstrate you are the perfect candidate for the job for which you are applying will make you attractive to your potential employer.

WRITING AN EFFECTIVE RESUME

A resume is a one-page summary of your education, work experience, accomplishments, and interests. Usually, only a few job candidates who send in their resumes will get the opportunity to interview for a job. A great resume can make all the difference, so you should invest plenty of time and effort into making your resume work for you.

Components of an Effective Resume

Good resumes share a few key characteristics: they are clear, concise, accurate, and free of any spelling and grammar errors. They include all relevant and necessary information; they are short (usually only one page) and to the point; and they have been carefully proofread to eliminate grammatical errors and typos. As you prepare your resume, keep in mind that you shouldn't try to include everything you have ever done. The point of an effective resume is to highlight the job experience you have that qualifies you for the job for which you are applying. If you don't carefully plan out what you want to include, you may end up with information that is not relevant to the job opportunity and your most important qualifications and accomplishments will be less likely to stand out. And don't forget—presentation counts. You won't come across as professional if your resume is missing important information or is sprinkled with grammar or spelling mistakes.

A standard resume has the following sections:

▶ contact information
▶ objective
▶ education
▶ experience
▶ skills, accomplishments, interests, and/or associations
▶ references

Contact Information

At the top of your resume, include your name (this should stand out with either boldfacing or a slightly larger font size), your address, telephone number(s), and e-mail address. (You can also include a fax number if you have one.) The telephone number you use should be the number where you can be most easily reached during work hours; include a cell phone number if you are difficult to reach on a land line. Make sure that you have an e-mail address that sounds professional, like your name. For example, an address like crazygirl@hotmail.com doesn't sound professional.

Objective

Include a short sentence stating your objective, which is simply your employment goal. The objective is your purpose in sending the resume—to get employment of a specific type or in a specific setting. The following are examples of objective statements.

▶ To teach art to preschool children.
▶ Employment in education of young children with special needs.
▶ To obtain a position as a program developer in a Montessori school.

Notice that the objectives listed above are very specific. Generally you should tailor your resume to the position you are applying for. This topic will be discussed further in a subsequent section.

Education

In this section, you should include any certificates or degrees you hold, starting with the most recent. State your program major and minor, if applicable. Include the name and location of the institution from which you received your degree and the month and year in which you received the degree. For example:

▶ **A.A. in Early Childhood Education**, CUNY Kingsborough Community College, Brooklyn, New York, May 2002.
If you are still studying, you can include the degree you will receive and the date you expect to receive it, as follows:
▶ **Certificate in Infant and Toddler Care**, Bellevue Community College, Bellevue, Washington. Expected May 2003.
Here, you can also include any licenses you hold and the states the licenses are valid in.

If you do not have a lot of work experience that is relevant to early childhood education, in this section you can also list some special or advanced course or courses you have taken or projects you have worked on. Remember to include your GPA when you are embarking on a first job; as you grow in professional endeavors over the years, you may drop this information, if you so choose.

Job Experience

Here you should list the relevant jobs you have held, starting with the most recent one first. Include:

▶ title for of your position (for example, *student teacher*)
▶ the name of the institution you worked for (for example, *The Playroom*)
▶ the location (city and state) of the institution (for example, *Miami, FL*)
▶ when you worked there (for example, *Summer 2000* or *Jan.–Sept. 2001*)

Then briefly describe your responsibilities and accomplishments at that job. Avoid using *I*. Try to use action words such as *implemented*, *improved*, *managed*, and *trained*, as well as any early childhood buzz words, such as *whole language approach, peer coaching/mentoring, outcome-based and performance-based education.*

If you feel that you don't have enough relevant work experience, you can include any jobs in which you developed communication or interpersonal skills, or any other skills that could be useful in your early childhood education job. In this section you can also include volunteer work. Don't forget babysitting—if you have supported yourself as a babysitter, even in high school, this counts as valid childcare experience.

Other Sections: Skills, Accomplishments (or Honors/Awards), Interests, and Associations

These additional sections allow you to include information about what makes you unique: your special skills and interests, your individual accomplishments and affiliations. In these sections, you can include any extracurricular activities you participated in, such as being a part of a swim team or volleyball team. You can list specific computer skills you have, including the programs you can use, as this is always an asset. And you can also include your interests and special skills, such as Web page design, playing piano, singing, speaking a foreign language. Who knows—maybe the place you will be applying to needs some extra help with their website. Perhaps a teacher who can organize a musical celebration for the holidays would be appreciated.

If you belong to any professional organizations or if you have won an award or recognition (such as being on the Dean's list), you should include it here. List the month or year in which you joined the association (or use the phrase "Member since _____") and include the date (month/year) in which you won the award.

Remember to keep these sections short, but be sure to include something that gives you a unique face and distinguishes you from other applicants. Don't include all four sections unless you have useful information to include in each. (That is, don't include a section for "Associations" and write "none"—instead, just omit the section entirely.)

References

Your references are your current or former employers, instructors, or other adults who can vouch for your skills, integrity, personality, and work ethic.

Pick individuals who know you well, who like you, and who are impressed with your work.

Some jobs will require you to supply the references with your resume. In that case you can note at the end of the resume that the references are attached or enclosed. Then, on a separate sheet, with your name and contact information on top, list your references. Include how they know you, their names, job title, and contact information.

Usually three references are enough, unless otherwise specified. If you are not specifically asked to supply references, at the end of your resume you could just write, "References available upon request." Always ensure that the references are available to provide information on your behalf and that they are aware of being listed by you.

Reckless or Reliable References

There are several key questions prospective employers like to ask your references, so be sure that the people you supply as references will answer these questions positively. They often ask about your:

- Ability to get the job done—Can the employer rely on you to do a job well and on time?
- Ability to work with others—Do you get along well with coworkers? Are you an effective team member? A good leader?
- Stability—How do you react to stress, difficult situations?
- Weaknesses—What are your major drawbacks? How do they affect your work?

It is important for your references to know specifically what position you are seeking. It may be a good idea to let your references know exactly what the responsibilities of the position are and remind them of your experience in those areas. That way it will be easier for them to address your abilities that relate to the particular job when they are called. NEVER use an individual's name as a reference without first getting approval, and only include people who will give you a good reference!

The following page provides a list of references.

Jennifer Nelson
86 Bridgeview Street
Brooklyn, NY 11217
718-555-5151

REFERENCES:

Student Teaching:
Chris Chan—Director
Riverside Weekday Preschool
New York, NY
212-555-8503

Nanny for children of:
Mary and Bob Eastman, parents of 3-year old Sean
New York, NY
212-555-4512

CPR Instructor:
Connie Gold
Supervisor, Family Prevention Programs
AIC Medical Center
Brooklyn, NY
718-555-8234

Formatting Your Resume

Your resume is not a place where you should show off your creativity—don't get fancy with tons of colors, fonts, or graphics. You can always show your creative side by including interesting lesson plans in your portfolio. The resume should be a neat and easy-to-read summary of your education, work experience, and accomplishments. Here are some general guidelines for formatting your resume so that it is clear and easy to follow.

- Use standard $8\frac{1}{2}$ by 11-inch white or ivory colored paper.
- Use a conservative, readable font, such as Times New Roman or Helvetica.
- Make the font large enough (typically 12 point) so that it is easy to read.
- Emphasize your name by making it slightly larger (e.g., 14 point font) and/or boldfaced.
- Include blank lines ("white space") between sections, so that the resume doesn't look crammed and it is easy to distinguish between sections.
- Make sure that your formatting is consistent throughout the resume. If, for example, you are italicizing the dates of your employment for one job, do the same for all of them. If you are boldfacing the title of one section, do that for all of them.

What Your Resume Should Not Include

It is illegal for employers to discriminate based on sex, race, nationality, religion, age, or family status. Don't include personal information of that sort in your resume. Also, don't include your desired or previous salary and reasons for leaving your former jobs, unless specifically instructed to do so. Listing a specific salary can eliminate you from the pool of potential candidates before an employer even finishes your resume.

On the next two pages you will find sample resumes. These are only models, presented to give you an idea of what kind of information can be included in a resume and how it can be presented. Your resume may be very different, but you should stick to the general guidelines presented in this chapter.

Min Culkin

427 16th St., Apt 1A, Brooklyn, NY 11215
Telephone: 718-555-5117
E-mail: mtea01@email.edu

OBJECTIVE:
To teach in a public early childhood center.

EDUCATION:
Master of Science, Early Childhood Education
Teachers College, Columbia University, New York, NY (expected June 2003).
Bachelor of Science, Early Childhood/Elementary Education
Frostburg State University, Frostburg, MD (June 2001).

EXPERIENCE:
West Side Montessori School, *New York, NY*
(Jan.–June 2000) Student Teacher
- Lessons for 3–5 year old class.
- Set up a musical theater performance in which all students participated.
- Organized a book fair.

Philmont Training Center, *Cimmaron, NM*
(Summer 1999) Program Counselor (Group Leader)
- Developed weekly activities for children and adults of all ages.
- Led and coordinated overnight backpacking trips and programs for youth.

Language Associates, *Frostburg, MD*
(Sept. 1998–June 1999) Personal Aide
- Assisted in feeding and changing a seven-year-old autistic girl.
- Practiced exercises with child as prescribed by her therapist.
- Wrote weekly reports on her progress.

MEMBERSHIPS AND RELATED SKILLS:
Member of National Association for the Education of Young Children.
Children's Literature Conference, 1999.
CPR, First Aid, and Lifeguard Certification.
Fluent in Spanish.

INTERESTS:
Playing violin, downhill skiing, and Web page design.

References available upon request.

Jazz Myn
427 16th St., Apt 1A, Brooklyn NY 11215
Phone: (H) 718-555-5117;
E-mail: jmyn01@email.edu

OBJECTIVE:
My Objective is to find a Job in Childhood.

EDUCATION:
I got my Bachelor of Science in Early Childhood/Elementary Education
Frostburg State University, Frostburg, MD (June 2001). My GPA was 2.5
I hope to go back to school soon to get my Masters because I love
children.

EXPERIENCE:
Here are some things I did:
Student Teacher
3-5 year old classes.
I observed and helped in many school districts and many grade levels in
order to develop a well rounded understanding of how different class-
rooms operate.
Philmont Training Center, *Cimmaron, NM*
(Summer 1999) Program Counselor (Group Leader)
I played with children and adults of all ages.
I also went on overnight backpacking trips with youth.
Pete's Ice Cream Shop, *Frostburg, MD*
(Sept. 1998–June 1999) Salles Associate
I sold ice cream to customers, including children.
I was in charge of organizing birthday parties for children.
I was accountable for the money and I decorated the window so we had
more customers.

OTHER:
I'm a member of National Association for the Education of Young
Children.
I went to Children's Literature Conference, 1999.
I have CPR, First Aid and Lifeguard Certification.
I'm fluent in Spanish

INTERESTS:
Playing violin, downhill skiing and Internet.

REFERENCES:
Available upon request.

Evaluating the Resumes

The two resumes contain very similar information, but you have guessed correctly if thought that the first one was more professional. Indeed, Min Culkin seems to have more education and more relevant experience than Jazz Myn. But that is not the only factor that makes the first resume better. Compare the two resumes carefully. What problems do you notice with Jazz Myn's resume? List them in the space below.

_____

_____

_____

_____

You may have noticed the following weaknesses in Jazz Myn's resume:

1. **Careless errors.** "Salles Associate" is a very obvious misspelling spelling for a "Sales Associate." In fact, this mistake is one that the spell checker can catch. Typos and writing mistakes on the resume show carelessness—something employers don't like to see. Spell-check your resume. Then give it to several trusted friends or family members who can catch mistakes, such as using *its* instead of *it's*.

2. **Too many busy fonts.** A resume shouldn't look like graffiti. The e-mail address on Jazz Myn's resume is hardly readable. Use only one font throughout, two at most. If you use two, use one for section headings and the other for text.

3. **The word "I" is used excessively.** It is *your* resume, so it is obvious that you are the one whose activities are outlined. You should not include *I*, it is preferable to use action verbs, like Min does in his resume.

4. **Poor objective.** The objective is too general. A prospective employer can tell that Jazz did not take much time formulating a specific objective.

5. **Unimpressive GPA.** The GPA of 2.5 is not very impressive and should not be included (unless it is a specified requirement in the job advertisement).

6. **Gaps in logic.** Going back to school for a master's degree is admirable and can be included in the resume. However, loving children isn't directly connected to getting a degree, as one can love children and not get a degree, as well as get a degree and not love children. This gap in logic contributes to her weak resume.

7. **Wasting valuable space.** The sentence "Here are some things I did" is superfluous, as the title "Experience" already suggests that a list of jobs will follow. You only have one page to highlight your experience, so you don't want to waste space with unnecessary sentences.

8. **Information gaps.** The location and time of the student teacher job experience is not listed. Even if the experience was at several different schools, the county and state could be given.

9. **Lack of specific examples.** The description under the student teacher experience is very wordy, and at the same time, it doesn't say much. How did Jazz help? Specific examples of helping in the classroom would be more informative.

10. **Ineffective explanation of experience.** The program counselor experience is described as if the counselor was just one of the participants who went along playing and backpacking with everyone else. The reader of the resume doesn't get the sense that the counselor had any responsibility. It is more effective to say "led, organized, and supervised overnight backpacking trips."

11. **Wordiness.** Overall the language of the resume could be more concise. For example, "I was accountable for the money and I decorated the window so we had more customers" could be broken up into several bulleted items such as
    - Handled sales transactions
    - Designed and decorated store windows
    - Implemented strategies to increase sales

12. **Crowded format.** The resume is too crammed together and it needs more white space.

With this feedback, Jazz could revise her resume as follows.

Jazz Myn
427 16th St., Apt 1A, Brooklyn, NY 11215
Phone: (H) 718-555-5117
E-mail: jmyn01@email.edu

OBJECTIVE:
To work in a small daycare center.

EDUCATION:
Bachelor of Science in Early Childhood/Elementary Education
Frostburg State University, Frostburg, MD (June 2001)
Plan to pursue an MS in early childhood education.

EXPERIENCE:
Dragonfly Early Childhood Center, *Westchester, NY*
(January–June 2001) Student Teacher 3–5 year old classes
- Designed programs to increase interaction among children.
- Developed demonstrations to teach science to children.
- Organized an exhibition of children's art.

Philmont Training Center, *Cimmaron, NM*
(Summer 1999) Program Counselor (Group Leader)
- Organized games for children and adults of all ages.
- Led overnight backpacking trips for youth.

Pete's Ice Cream Shop, *Akron, OH*
(Sept. 1998–June 1999) Sales Associate
- Sold ice cream.
- Organized birthday parties for children.
- Handled all money transactions.
- Decorated the window, which resulted in increased sales.

OTHER:
- Member of National Association for the Education of Young Children.
- Attended Children's Literature Conference, 1999.
- CPR, First Aid, and Lifeguard Certification.
- Fluent in Spanish.

INTERESTS:
Playing violin, downhill skiing and Web design.

References available upon request.

Clearly, the revised resume looks and sounds more professional, and Jazz is much more likely to land an interview.

After you write your own resume, revise it several times yourself. Then give it to at least three other adults for feedback. If there is a career office that you can go to (for example, in your school), ask the career counselor for suggestions. Then, taking the suggestions into account, revise it again, and repeat the process until several people can agree that you have created an effective, professional resume.

Modifying Your Resume to Fit a Job Description

Your resume should always be truthful. Many institutions make it a point to check the information you provide, so you shouldn't twist the facts, even if you think it would be more likely to get you an interview. However, you may emphasize different accomplishments and skills depending upon where you apply. For example, if the job description requires experience with technology, you can highlight your computer skills on your resume by listing the programs in which you are proficient, those with which you are familiar, and include any jobs or experience that required extensive use of computers. If, on the other hand, the ideal candidate for the job is someone with great communication skills, list being a staff member on a childcare newsletter at your school, writing children's stories, or having held a job where you were required to write reports and give presentations. Your objective should also be modified specifically to target the job you are applying for.

Helpful Hints

Your resume should be truthful, to the point, readable, and informative. It is not very difficult to check the information you include on your resume. Play up your skills and assets and don't be too shy to list your accomplishments, but don't make things up. All your statements and job descriptions should be specific and clear. Avoid being vague or wordy. Make sure that the resume is spell-checked, organized into sections and easy to read. Include the most recent and relevant information, listing accomplishments and skills that are pertinent to the job you are applying for.

It may be worthwhile to writing a resume that includes *all* the jobs and activities you have held, listing *all* your responsibilities and the skills you have picked up along the way, without worrying about the one page limit. This will allow you to edit that resume based on the job description—keep the experiences you think that the prospective employers will value and delete the job experiences that do not relate to this job until you can fit everything on one page. You may also want to have a copy of a standard, more generic, resume that you can give out at a job fair or post on the Web.

THE COVER LETTER

The cover letter is just as important as the resume. It is a business style letter that expresses your interest in the job, describes where you have heard about it, why you are qualified for it, and briefly introduces your qualifications to the employer. Its purpose is to get the employer to look at your resume and consider you for a specific position.

A good cover letter is short and to the point; it should highlight the specific skills that make you an excellent candidate for the position, but it should not try to summarize your resume. Your cover letter is an important introduction, but it's just an introduction. Save the details for your resume.

It is best to address a cover letter to a specific person, rather than to a "Dear Sir" or "Dear Madam." If a name is not available, try to find it on the Internet or call your prospective employer to find out to whom to address a cover letter for a job application. As in any business letter, you should include your address, the recipient's address, and the date. You should also list the materials you are including, such as your resume, references, and so on. Don't forget to sign the letter at the end.

The next page contains an example of an effective cover letter.

Ana B. Elli
225 Raven Place
Allentown, NJ 18104

May 23, 2002

Ellen A. Pole
Program Director
Fortunato Weekday Preschool
Bayside, NY 11361

Dear Dr. Pole:

Yoshio Itagaki, a career counselor at NYU, alerted me to the opening
you have available at the Fortunato Weekday Preschool. I was especially
excited to hear of the opening since the job requirements match my
own skills and traits: patience, creativity, ability to handle difficult
situations, belief in parental involvement in a child's education, and above
all a great love for children. Along with this letter, I have also enclosed
my resume, which outlines examples of these traits, along with a sample
of my writing—a term paper entitled "Learning through Song."

The job environment at Fortunato closely matches my ideal—small
classrooms, a tight community, a diverse student body. I am extremely
supportive of children of different ages playing together, helping one
another to learn.

I would love to discuss the job opportunity with you at greater length.
Please feel free to contact me at 201-555-4875. I look forward to an
opportunity to meet with you; thank you for your time and
consideration.

Sincerely,

Ana B. Elli

Ana B. Elli

Enclosure.

Sending the Resume and Cover Letter

It is important that you send your resume and cover letter in the way in which you were instructed. If you were told to fax it, then fax it; don't send it electronically or by regular mail.

Many employers will now accept resumes and cover letters electronically. Make sure that you have a version of the resume that you can send electronically without affecting the layout. As a test, you can send your resume to a friend and check whether the file transfer changed the original layout.

Electronic Resume

Some employers will ask you for an electronic version of your resume. Most likely the file will need to be in ASCII or Rich Text format. You could also create a Web page with your resume that your potential employers could visit.

Here are some guidelines for formatting the electronic resume

- Set the margins to 6.5 inches to ensure that the text won't automatically wrap to the next line (unless you want it to).
- Use a basic, 12-point text font, such as Times New Roman.
- Avoid using bullets or other symbols. Instead of a bullet, use an asterisk ('*') or a dash ('-').
- Use a spellchecker and then proofread the document carefully yourself.
- Avoid using multiple columns, tables, or charts within your document.

THE INTERVIEW

Mission accomplished. You have landed an interview. Your next mission is preparing for the interview so that you can land the job. In the next section, you will find some guidelines on how to get ready for the interview. Preparation will decrease the chance of unpleasant surprises and will make you feel more confident.

Setting Up the Interview

Every contact you have with a potential employer is an opportunity to leave a good impression. One of the first contacts you will have is when setting up the interview. The interviewer will most likely call you to find out when you are available. Try not to be too fussy about the times. You should also make sure that during the time of your job search you have an answering machine or voicemail with a simple, professional message and that you always answer the phone politely. Avoid long, goofy messages or music. A simple message that states, "You have reached Jane Smith. Please leave a message and I will return your call," or a similar, simple greeting is the safest way to go. If you miss the interviewer's call, be sure to call back as soon as possible, introducing yourself clearly and explaining that you are returning the call to set up a time for an interview. Here are some other guidelines:

- ▶ Have your planner and a pen handy to set up a good time for the interview.
- ▶ Try to be flexible.
- ▶ Note the date, time, and location of the interview and be sure to get the name of the main person who will be interviewing you.
- ▶ Ask if you need to bring any documents or other supporting materials with you.

Preparing for the Interview

The key to a successful interview is extensive preparation. Reduce the possibility of surprises and mishaps and you will do just fine. You can best prepare by:

- ▶ Getting as much information about the job before the interview—research the school or speak to people in your network who may have knowledge of it.
- ▶ Anticipating the questions the interviewer may ask you—see pages 116–117 for a list of common interview questions.

► Thinking about how you will answer those questions—have a friend or family member rehearse with you and give you feedback before the real interview.

If you get nervous on interviews or if you have never interviewed for a job before, it would be helpful to have mock interviews with a friend or career counselor.

Think Ahead!

Preparation is the key to a successful interview. Don't leave things to chance and hope that the last-minute adrenaline rush will get you the job. If an hour before the interview you are shining your shoes, ironing your clothes, and looking for directions to the interview, chances are that you will get there stressed out and probably late. Do whatever you can as far in advance as possible. Practice answering common interview questions. That way, on the day of the interview you will be more calm and will have extra time just in case there are traffic jams, flat tires, or broken zippers.

Research the Early Childhood Education (ECE) Center and the Area

The more you know about your potential employer before your interview, the better. You will be more comfortable and confident, and you will be able to ask more meaningful questions during your interview.

One way to get information about the workplace is by visiting the center *before* the interview. This will give you a chance to check out the location, determine how to get there, estimate your travel time, and find out where you can park.

If you get a chance, talk to some parents while you are there. Ask them what they like and don't like about the center and what a typical day at the center looks like for their children. Ask them about their concerns and suggestions for improvement. You may also want to talk to a few kids. This will not necessarily help you answer any interview questions, but it may help you come up with questions to ask the interviewer.

Taking an interest in the center and touring the center before the interview will show the interviewer that you are serious and genuinely interested in getting the job. It will also help you determine whether the job is right for you. And being able to picture yourself at the job will help you respond to questions during the interview.

Be Informed

As an ice-breaker, the interviewer may first engage in casual chit-chat. It may be about the weather or about current events. You won't be expected to enter a heated political debate—and, in fact, it is probably in your best interest not to discuss anything too controversial that is not directly related to the job opportunity. But you should be aware of major world events and the issues facing the community in which you may be working. Follow the news on education policies, budget cuts or increases, trends in education, and so on. Having an overview of the trends and changes in policy in your field can give you an additional conversation topic with the interviewer and will demonstrate that you care about the issues that affect your career.

Appearance Counts

You want to project an image that is clean, neat, and professional. At the same time, in a field where your personality is so important and the dress code is far more casual than in the business world, you have greater freedom in how you present yourself. So while you should dress professionally, you don't have to dress as if for an interview with a Fortune 500 corporation. The standard, conservative blue suit would be fine, but you can also choose an outfit that better fits your personal style and matches the personality of the center. Of course, your hair should be clean, neatly cut and brushed; your clothing should be ironed, your shoes shined, and your nails cut and clean. You will get a better idea of how to dress by visiting the center; look for clues to the level of formality and dress accordingly. And always remember that in an interview, it is better to be overdressed, rather than underdressed.

In any case, it is wise to avoid clothing that is too revealing or flashy, such as a low-cut blouse or a neon-green suit. Especially since you will be around small children, don't wear dangling jewelry of any kind (true for both men and women), and excessive makeup can often create a negative impression. A portfolio folder or briefcase should suffice to carry your interview materials. Women should err on the side of smaller purses. If you will be wearing nylons, you may want to bring an extra pair with you, so that you can change if you get a run as you are getting out of your car or off the bus.

What to Bring

You may be asked to fill out an application for the job before your interview, and most applications require that you provide past residence addresses, the addresses of the schools you went to, and addresses of your former jobs. You may also be asked for your work papers, Social Security card, and Alien Registration Card or visa (if applicable). Have that information and those documents available. You may also bring a portfolio of materials that reflect your teaching personality and experience.

Portfolio

A portfolio is a compilation of materials that demonstrate your experience as a teacher and illustrate your teaching philosophy and style. A portfolio can include the following:

- a statement of your philosophy of education
- a statement listing methods used in behavior management
- lesson plans that you have created
- samples of adaptations or accommodations for students with learning challenges
- pictures of a learning setting you have created
- pictures of children (and you)

Arrive Ahead of Time

Come to the interview a little bit ahead of time. There is no excuse for coming to an interview late. When you start working, a whole class full of children and their parents will count on you to be on time every day. Being late to the interview will suggest that you may sometimes come late to work, possibly leaving the children without sufficient care.

Meeting the Interviewer

When you meet the interviewer, or really anyone at a potential workplace, be calm. Look the person in the eye, smile, and shake hands firmly. Introduce yourself and try to commit to memory the names of the people you are introduced to. (Tip: Repeating a person's name when they introduce themselves is a good way to help you remember: "Nice to meet you, Tim.") Exchange a common greeting such as "I'm pleased to meet you". Remember that the interview is not an interrogation, but just a meeting designed to see if there is a good match between you and the job. The interviewer is looking for a worthwhile candidate, just as you are looking for a worthwhile job, so you have nothing to fear. The person interviewing you may be your future colleague. Be polite, but also be yourself.

Face-to-Face: The Interview

Typically, in the interview, you will answer and ask questions. Prepare for both and the interview will be much less stressful. Maintain eye contact throughout the interview and avoid nervous gestures, such as tapping your fingers, swinging your foot, and playing with your hair.

To prepare for the interview, try to anticipate the questions you might be asked. List as many as you can on paper and then think about what you would answer to those questions. Don't write down or memorize your answers—just have a general idea of what you would say.

There are two basic categories of interview questions: *professional* questions and *situational* questions. Professional questions are those pertaining to your ability to perform the duties of the job—questions about what you are like, why you want the job, and what experience you have in early childhood education. Situational questions are hypothetical questions designed to see how you would respond to certain situations and are usually a little more difficult. Alternatively, the interviewer can ask you to describe what you already have done in a given difficult situation. Rarely, the interviewer will ask you a third type of question to test your knowledge of material you learned in a course. For example, you may get a question about stages of development. Your interview may include just one of these categories, or a mixture of all of these.

Professional Questions

Here are some sample professional questions:

1. What are your weaknesses?
2. Why do you want to work in ECE?
3. What is your education philosophy?
4. Describe the classroom you would like to teach in.

5. I see on your resume that you went to a Children's Literature conference. What did you think of it?
6. What do you see yourself doing five years from now?
7. Who was your favorite teacher/instructor and why?
8. I see that your major was originally economics. What made you change it?
9. How would you motivate your students? (Name three different ways.)

There are no right or wrong answers to any of these questions. Answer honestly. Try to be enthusiastic, positive, and confident, without appearing too full of yourself. Your replies should indicate that you feel qualified for the job, and that you have many accomplishments, but not that you are perfect.

When you are discussing your strengths, it is a good idea to tell a short anecdote to elaborate, rather than just listing a trait. Saying "I'm patient," for example, doesn't tell the interviewer much about you. The following response would give the interviewer much more information about you and about what patience means to you:

> I'd have to say that my strength when working with children is patience. I'm the oldest of four children, and between helping to raise my brothers and sister and working as a nanny for two years, I've learned that most children are willing to cooperate if you just give them a chance. That means being patient enough to allow them to shift their focus so that they're ready to work with you.

When talking about your weaknesses, try to list a trait that you can cast in a positive light. Don't say "I'm lazy" or "I'm selfish." Try the following:

> I'm a bit of a perfectionist. Once I was working on a presentation on whales for a class where I was a student teacher. I found a picture of a whale that I scanned and imported into PowerPoint. For some reason, the scan kept being a little to the side. I don't think the children would have noticed or cared if the picture wasn't perfectly horizontal, but I spent an hour and a half trying to get it perfectly aligned. Now, I try to ask myself ahead of time how much time I can put into a task and decide ahead of time when good is good enough.

At worst this anecdote will make you sound slightly compulsive, but you are also showing that you take your work seriously, that you don't want to do a sloppy job, and that you are aware of and are working on ways to control this weakness. Notice that this story very casually and naturally weaves in some computer skills.

You may also be asked about your former jobs, including why you left them. Be prepared to answer those questions in a positive manner. For example, you will probably come off as a shallow or hard-to-please employee if you say, "I left because I didn't like the director." Instead, you might say,

> I left because I felt that the center expected behavior from the children that was not age appropriate.

Be prepared to give a specific example to support what you have said here; your interviewer may be interested, for example, in what sort of behavior you expect from children. So, when answering questions, be specific, giving examples that will enable the interviewer to understand your point. Be honest and have a positive attitude.

Situational Questions

Here are some sample hypothetical (situational) questions:

1. What would you do if a parent complained that his child does not have any friends?

2. What would you do if a child broke her tooth while playing in your class?

3. Tell me about a time when you thought that a coworker with whom you were working didn't contribute. How did you handle it?

4. How would you manage a child who disrupts the class constantly?

As with personal questions, there is no right or wrong answer. Think back to similar situations you have encountered and how you handled them. You want to show your potential employer that you are not afraid to make decisions and resolve conflicts, or act quickly and responsibly in a crisis. If you think you would handle the situation differently now that you have more experience, say so. Remember, the interviewer is not going to judge you based only on your *solution* to the problem but he or she will also consider your *attitude* toward the problem.

Difficult Questions

If a question really catches you off guard (which it shouldn't if you prepare well), take a breath and admit that "That's a tough one" or "I need to think about that for a moment." This will give you a few moments to think. You could describe how you would react, list several possible solutions to the problem, and then pick the best one. Don't dwell on it too much though, because you want to have time for other questions that hopefully will be easier. If you are really caught off-guard by a situational question, you could answer that you would feel most comfortable consulting your supervisor before doing anything. Keep in mind that this is not a good answer if there is a medical or other urgent emergency. Also, remember that you want to show your potential employer that you can handle problems on your own. But admitting that you sometimes need help shows both modesty and respect for others with more experience and authority.

Inappropriate Questions

If a question makes you uncomfortable, it could be for good reason. There are some questions that an interviewer should *not* ask you. These include questions about your marital status, children, religion, and sexual preference. If asked directly or indirectly about any of these, you have the right to politely refuse to answer or change the topic. For example if the interviewer asks you

"Do you live alone?" you could answer "Two years ago, I spent a summer living with a family with a set of three year-old twins." In this way you acknowledge that you have heard the question, but you are not revealing any information about your current situation. At the same time, you are shifting the focus to where it should be—your job experience. Most likely, your interviewer will be a trained individual, aware of what are appropriate and inappropriate questions for an interview, so this will not be an issue.

Asking Questions of Your Own

Usually, the interviewer will tell you a little bit about the job and then invite you to ask questions. Of course, you will want to know how you will be compensated, but at this stage, it is best to stick to questions that show your general interest in the job. Listen attentively to the answers, without interrupting. You can ask a follow-up question once the interviewer is done talking.

Sample questions to ask:

1. What will my responsibilities be at this job?
2. What does a typical workday look like?
3. What is the extent of parental involvement in the school?
4. I noticed that there is a children's art exhibition in the main hallway. Will I be able to organize an event like that?
5. How do teachers typically handle conflicts between children?
6. How do you evaluate teachers?
7. What is the school's philosophy of education?
8. What do you enjoy about working here?

Ending the Interview

When the interview is over, thank your interviewers for their time, and shake hands firmly. Express your interest in the job and ask when you can expect to hear from them. You shouldn't ask about salary or benefits at this point or at any time during the interview. It may also be a good idea to give the interviewers something to keep—a sample of your writing that shows your communication skills, a part of your portfolio, a disk with some of your works—something that demonstrates your unique qualifications the interviewers can look at when you leave and remember you by.

The Phone Interview

Occasionally, employers will first want to conduct an over-the-phone interview to screen candidates before they invest time in an in-person interview. A phone interview generally will be shorter than an in-person interview, but probably will involve similar types of questions about your personality, skills, experiences, and educational philosophy.

You can prepare for a phone interview in the same way you would for an in-person interview. Before the phone interview, make sure your phone is not busy. Disable call-waiting and remove any potential distractions or interruptions so that you give the interviewer your full attention. The good thing about phone interviews is that you only need to sound good. You could be wearing your slippers, pajamas, or your hair could be a mess and the interviewer wouldn't ever know it!

Thank You Letter

Following up after the interview is extremely important. You can prepare a stamped envelope and the beginning of a thank you letter even before the interview. That way you can send the letter right after your interview.

Sending the thank you letter gives you an opportunity to remind your potential employer that you are interested in the job and that you appreciate the time they spent with you. You can also use the thank you letter to remind the interviewers of your qualifications and how the job fits nicely with your skill set. It is also a good idea to mention something you discussed in the interview to remind your potential employer who you are. Here is a sample thank you letter:

Virginia Ateh
86 College Rd.
Athens, GA 34000

Dorothy Schultz
Director, Popeye Preschool
54 Pacific St.
Atlanta, GA 34000

Dear Ms. Shultz:

My visit to Popeye Preschool was very enjoyable. I enjoyed visiting your beautiful environment for children to grow in and I could easily picture myself working there. I am especially impressed with the independence you are fostering in the children. In the class I visited, I sensed a feeling of freedom and eagerness to explore among the students.

My philosophy of child development, where independence plays a central role, will enable me to fit into the environment you have created at Popeye. Furthermore, my creativity and love of games will contribute to that environment and stimulate the children to learn while having fun.

Thank you for taking the time to meet with me and for giving me a tour. I'm looking forward to hearing from you soon and meeting with you again.

Sincerely,

Virginia Ateh

Virginia Ateh

In Action

Once you are deemed to be a very strong candidate for the job, you may be invited to prepare a lesson, teach a class, supervise infants and toddlers, or run story or circle time, so that the employer can see your skills in action. If you have come this far, you have come a long way, but you are still not off the hook. No matter how much experience you have, don't think you can just walk into a center or school and just wing it. This step is an important part of the interview process, and one you need to prepare for, just as you did for the interview.

One way to prepare for teaching a class is to meet the class you will be teaching and to consult with their regular teacher before you actually teach them. Meeting the children will give you an idea of how large the class is, how old they are, how lively they are, what their relationships with the teacher and each other are like. Also, if they meet you ahead of time, they will be more comfortable with you when you come to teach them. Their regular teacher can fill you in on what they have been learning about, and perhaps can suggest a lesson for you to teach. Try to come up with an activity that will be both engaging and educational and that will involve all of the children in the class.

Summary

Now that you have a better idea of how to write a resume and a cover letter, how to prepare for an interview, and how to follow up with a thank you letter to land a job, you are ready to learn how to succeed in the classroom once you have landed the job in Chapter 6.

THE INSIDE TRACK

Who: Marco Annunziata
What: Creative Writing Teacher
Where: Bronx, NY

INSIDER'S STORY

When I graduated from college, I knew exactly what I wanted to do: I wanted to be a writer. Unfortunately, there are no entry-level positions for young novelists, and I needed to find a job that would let me support myself and give me time to write. I always thought that teaching sounded like a good idea, but I didn't have a degree in education and I wasn't certified to teach. A few months later I was talking to my friend and he told me that because of the shortage of teachers in New York City, the Board of Education was hiring teachers without certification for certain school districts. To me, this sounded like a great idea—I could work as a teacher and see if was something to make a career out of. I thought that I'd have plenty of time to write; it sounded pretty good to me.

I was hired as a creative writing teacher in an elementary school in the Bronx. At the outset, it seemed like an ideal job for me. I was what is called "a module" teacher. Basically, I was like an art teacher, except with words.

There is a misconception among people who aren't familiar with the teaching profession that teachers have it easy—they have early hours, they have summers off, all those holidays—but in your first week as a teacher you quickly realize that is all a myth. Nobody works harder than teachers, especially first-year teachers. The actual teaching is the easiest part of the job. By the time you finish your lesson plans, grade your papers, and figure out how to actually manage a class full of 35 seven-year-olds who have no writing skills, you barely have time to breathe. I don't think I wrote even a haiku for myself in the first few months I was adjusting to teaching young children.

The school in which I was placed was in a low-income neighborhood in the inner city, and the amount of students who came from broken families was astounding. On my first Parent-Teacher Night, only five parents came to visit my classroom. The climate of apathy in the community was shocking. It filtered down from the parents to the students; therefore, keeping control of my classes was often impossible. Most of my students, even the youngest ones, couldn't have cared less whether they passed or failed, and many of their social skills were non-existent—all these problems translated into classroom chaos. The thing about the whole situation that really upset me was that I felt like I was babysitting more than anything else. It was especially frustrating because the kids who were bright and wanted to learn were being neglected because I had to spend a large portion of class time keeping the unruly kids in line.

As I learned how to manage my classes better (I had many long mentoring sessions with my principal and other, more experienced, teachers), the kids' attitudes changed. Then I began to have many more positive interactions with the kids. You can really make a difference (especially in the inner city) in a child's emotional life. I saw a number of kids that were neglected in all aspects of life—at home, at school, socially. Recognizing that fact and then making a child realize that he or she is vital and important is a priceless privilege a teacher has, and one that shouldn't be taken lightly. Many times a teacher is the only person who even pays a bit of attention to a child. Once I got to know my kids through their writings, that insight helped me deal with their challenging behavior better.

During that difficult first year teaching in the Bronx, I learned that it takes a special type of person to be a teacher in the inner city; you have to have patience, a sense of purpose, and a serious love of teaching. Working that year I learned that there are teachers who really believe in the profession and want to make a difference helping young children learn and grow. These are the teachers from which I drew my own inspiration. What type of person are you? That's probably the most important question you should think about before committing to becoming a teacher.

CHAPTER six

HOW TO SUCCEED IN EARLY CHILDHOOD EDUCATION ONCE YOU HAVE LANDED THE JOB

THERE IS NO simple formula for on-the-job success, but there are many strategies you can use to help shorten your learning curve and make your first few weeks—not to mention the rest of your career—more successful. This chapter discusses the importance of understanding the written and unwritten expectations of your employer, your students, and their parents, and knowing who and when to ask for help. It also describes how to communicate effectively with parents and colleagues. You will also learn about resources for career advancement and professional development, the keys to classroom management, and the special challenges you may face in your career as an early childhood educator.

CONGRATULATIONS! You have had a successful interview and landed a great job—now you are ready to begin your career as an early childhood educator. Your preliminary work is finished; now, what can you do to help ensure your success in the classroom?

In any job, and especially in education, a successful start depends upon the right approach and the right attitude. No matter how much you learned in your certificate or degree program, and no matter how much experience you may already have caring for children, you are starting a new job—and that means you are headed for a learning curve, a period of major adjustment as you discover what it takes to succeed in your new position. As confident as you may feel about your abilities, you are entering a new environment with its own culture, and you will be working with a whole new group of people, including supervisors, colleagues, parents, and children. You will need to adapt quickly to this culture and make good use of your resources in order to be successful at your new job.

SCHOOL CULTURE: FINDING OUT AND FITTING IN

By the time you accept a job offer, you should already have a general sense of the culture of the school or center where you will work, including its philosophy, expectations of both employees and students, and the type of students enrolled at the school. If you were able to meet other teachers and talk with children and parents before beginning your new job, you may also have a general idea of the "personality" of the school and whether the program is tightly or loosely structured—for example, whether caregivers are encouraged to be affectionate with children or asked to refrain from physical contact. This personality is shaped largely by the written and unwritten expectations of the school and the personality of your supervisor(s) and colleagues.

Written Expectations

Before you begin working with children at your new job, you should receive one or more handbooks that document the policies and procedures of the center. If you don't get any written documentation before you begin, *ask for it*. If no written procedures exist, or if what exists seems unclear or insufficient, create your own documentation and review it with your supervisor. See "Policies and Procedures for Nannies" on page 129.

As you can imagine, it is critical for your on-the-job success—and the safety of the children—that you read these handbooks carefully and make sure that you understand, and follow, the employer's policies and procedures. You should know how the center expects you to handle everything from basic procedures (such as when to arrive and where to place your personal belongings) to emergency situations (such as serious injuries), which can arise, even on your very first day. Besides, the more familiar you are with policies and procedures, the more comfortable you will be when you start your new position.

After you review the center's written policies and procedures, make a list of any questions you have. Be sure to schedule time with your supervisor to review those questions *before* you begin supervising children.

What to Expect in Your Center's Handbook

Handbooks for early childhood educators may vary greatly from school to school and center to center, but you should expect your handbook to include information about the following kinds of policies and procedures (you can use this list as a guide if you need to create your own list of policies and procedures):

- arrival and departure time for staff
- arrival and departure time for children
- procedures for handling late arrivals and pick-ups
- procedures for food preparation and distribution
- cleaning responsibilities
- emergency procedures and phone numbers
- what information concerning children should be documented in writing, and how often
- what types of parent meetings are required, if any, and how often
- what types of staff meetings are required, and how often
- diaper changing and potty training procedures
- where to put personal belongings
- where to put children's belongings
- policies regarding breaks and meals
- healthcare and other benefits, including holidays, sick days, and vacation
- dress code for teachers
- Required membership in professional organizations and other requirements, such as certification in CPR

Policies and Procedures for Nannies

As a nanny, you will probably get most of your instructions about policies and procedures verbally rather than in writing. However, it is important to take those verbal instructions and put them down on paper. If you don't receive any documentation in writing from the parents of the children you will be caring for, create a detailed job description with the policies and procedures as you understand them. For example, will you still be paid if your employer decides to take a day off? How much notice must you give for a personal day? Can you take the child(ren) with you to personal appointments, such as a medical check-up? Exactly what household cleaning duties are you responsible for?

After you have finished, review your document with your employer as soon as possible. The best bet for on-the-job success is to know what is expected of you so you can meet—and exceed—those expectations.

Keys to Success

1. **Know what's expected of you.** Carefully review written expectations. Be observant and ask questions to determine unwritten expectations as quickly as possible.

2. *Surpass* **those expectations.** Once you have a good understanding of your employer's expectations, find ways to go beyond those expectations. Show initiative and dedication to both the center and its children. For example, there are always small tasks that don't really "belong" to anyone, such as reorganizing the bookshelf or labeling supplies. And there are many ways to exceed expectations when you are dealing with children. The more genuinely you care for them, and the more effort you put into helping them develop strong skills and healthy attitudes, the greater impact you will have on the children—and your career.

3. **Love what you do.** You have chosen early childhood education as a career because you enjoy working with children. It is important to remember that, especially on difficult days. It won't always be easy, and some days will be extremely challenging. But those days will be balanced by others in which you will see evidence that your hard work is paying off. You will be able to watch the children in your care learn and grow, developing important social and intellectual skills through your expert guidance.

Unwritten Expectations

Often as important as the written expectations are the unwritten expectations at your new place of employment. For example, according to your handbook, you may be expected to arrive by 8:30 each morning, but you may soon realize that all of your colleagues are in by 8:00 and that 8:30 is unofficially considered late. And although it may never be stated in writing, you may also be expected to send home written reminders about trips and special events, to bring a snack to share with your colleagues once every other week, or to organize a holiday pageant for the children.

To help you figure out these important unwritten expectations, **be observant** and **ask questions**. Especially in your first few weeks, pay extra careful attention to what your colleagues do. Note everything from when they arrive and how they dress to what kind of interactions they have with each other. And talk to your colleagues. Remember, people love to give advice. Don't be afraid to ask them questions geared toward helping you fit in to the school's culture, such as "What was it like for you when you first started?" This question gives your colleagues an opportunity to offer important information about unwritten expectations, share stories about mistakes they may have made as beginning early childhood educators, and describe ways in which the center may have changed over the years. It also gives them a chance to invite you to participate in social activities.

Here are some specific things you might ask about and observe, especially in the first few weeks:

- ▶ What happens on the first day of school? What special events or procedures are there in the first day/week? What sort of orientation is provided to parents and children?
- ▶ Are there any children with special needs?
- ▶ Do any of the children have certain habits or patterns that you should be aware of? Do any children have special fears or problems you should know about?
- ▶ Are there staff meetings to provide input regarding curriculum development? How can you get involved in curriculum development?
- ▶ What time do teachers normally arrive and depart?
- ▶ How do staff handle lunch? Do they often eat together?
- ▶ What records are kept of children's growth and behavior? How are they kept? How often do parents see them?
- ▶ How much interaction is there with parents at drop-off and pick-up time? How often do you have formal meetings with parents?

The Golden Rule:
Don't Be Afraid to Ask for Help

Your first few months of teaching can be filled with dilemmas, some of which you may have anticipated and, probably, many that you hadn't. You may feel alone, but you are not. *Every* new childcare provider faces problems—and so do experienced ones.

The good news is that you don't have to do it alone. Ask your colleagues for help. Share your questions and concerns with them. They have had similar experiences, they have probably made similar mistakes, and they are often a tremendous wealth of information as well as great sources of comfort and guidance. Turning to your colleagues for assistance can help you learn a lot faster, make friends more quickly, and become a more effective teacher.

A word of caution. At the same time, however, remember that *not all advice is good advice.* Though you shouldn't be afraid to turn to your colleagues for help, especially at first, be cautious about heeding all of the advice you are given. If something strikes you as wrong or illogical, check with your supervisor.

Whenever you address your supervisor, be careful not to point fingers. Don't say, for example, "Alex told me that it's all right to have a cup of coffee while the children are arriving in the morning. Is this true?" If you are not supposed to have hot drinks in the classroom, you may cause trouble for your colleague and quickly alienate someone who should be your ally. Instead, keep your colleague out of it: "Is it all right to have a cup of coffee while the children are arriving in the morning?" If your supervisor's response is the same as what your colleague advised, then you can give your colleague credit: "Great. That's what Alex said too, but I wanted to check with you first." In this way you show that you have taken the time to check on something about which you were unsure and that you know how to give credit when credit's due. If your supervisor's response is different from your colleague's, you have safeguarded your developing relationship with your colleague and shown your supervisor you recognize the importance of following proper procedure.

Finding Out Who's Who:
Hierarchy and Housekeeping at Your School or Center

Every organization has a certain hierarchy or chain of command among its employees. In an early childhood education center, you will typically have a director, an assistant director, a curriculum developer, a head teacher(s), teachers, assistant teachers, and support staff, including secretaries and administrative assistants. Some staff may be full time while others, particularly those who offer special services such as music or foreign language instruction, may work with the children two or three times a week, or only in the mornings.

To adapt to your center's culture, shorten your learning curve, and make the most of your colleagues' knowledge and experience, get to know who's who as quickly as possible. Who is responsible for what in the organization? For example, whom should you see if there is a problem with your paycheck? Whom should you talk to if you discover that a child has a food allergy? Whom should you see if you want to arrange a field trip or need some supplies? Remember, everyone in the center is a resource for you; the sooner you get to know each person and establish a good rapport, the smoother your transition, the fewer your problems, and the greater your chances for success.

Typical Hierarchy in Early Childhood Education

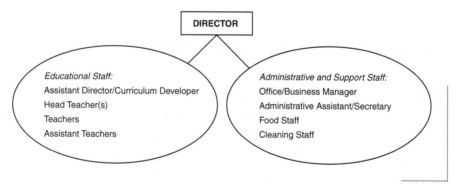

When to Go to the Director

You will be able to answer many questions and solve many problems on your own or by talking with administrative staff and your fellow teachers. For example, if you have a question about where to put soiled clothing, a fellow teacher or an administrative assistant can help you; there is certainly no need to go to your director. But there are other times when you should definitely seek the counsel of your supervisor. Make sure you go to the director:

▶ whenever there is an issue about a child's safety or well being, or a question about a fundamental principle of the school's philosophy.

▶ whenever you are unsure of whether you have handled a situation properly.

▶ whenever you have made a mistake that may have repercussions for the child or the school.

Don't let embarrassment or fear of reprimand keep you from discussing a problem or error. Admitting that you didn't handle something well or that you breached policy is the best way to find out how to handle the situation properly and regain any lost ground. On the other hand, attempting to hide a mistake or problem and hoping that it will either go unnoticed or fix itself can lead to disaster. Remember, you are the "new kid on the block"—you are *expected* to make mistakes. You are not expected to know everything, and you are not expected to know the right course of action every time. This knowledge comes with experience and expert guidance.

DEALING EFFECTIVELY WITH PARENTS

Unlike secondary school teachers who typically see parents only a few times each term, as an early childhood educator, you are more likely to see the parents of the children you care for just about every day. This gives you a unique opportunity to establish good relationships with parents and to keep them informed and involved.

Not surprisingly, having a good relationship with parents can dramatically enhance your effectiveness as caretaker of their children. The better parents feel about you, the more likely their children—even if they are infants—will have a positive attitude about being left in your care.

The key to building a strong relationship with parents (and with your colleagues) is **communication**. Here are some above-and-beyond strategies to help get you off to a good start:

▶ Take the time to introduce yourself to parents in writing when you begin your new job. Create a short, friendly flyer with information about your background and qualifications. Your goal should be to convey your personality along with your education and experience. Even just a few cheerful lines briefly describing your schooling, experience, and educational philosophy will help parents feel more comfortable about placing their children in your care.

YOUR CHILD HAS A NEW TEACHER!

Hi, I'm Tanya Reed, and I've just joined the faculty at Willowbrook Preschool and Childcare Center. I've been teaching 4-year-olds for eight years now and am very excited to be working here at Willowbrook. This is a school that fits my early childhood education philosophy perfectly. Here, children learn through play and choose their projects independently to build upon their interests and increase their self-esteem.

I've wanted to be a preschool teacher ever since I can remember, and I started working in a childcare center while I was still in high school. I soon earned my bachelor's degree in Early Childhood Education and am also certified to work with children with special needs. I've done research in children's literature and am even working on a children's book of my own.

This is an exciting time for me and I'm looking forward to getting to know you and your child. I can't wait for the learning and fun that's ahead!

Sincerely,

Tanya Reed

Tanya Reed

▶ Learn parents' names right from the start. Write them down if necessary and review them until you have them memorized. In fact, it is a good idea to post a chart with children and parent names in your room so that a substitute can address parents by name if you are absent. And don't hesitate to introduce yourself to parents of children in other classrooms. This demonstrates your interest in all the children in the school and gives you an edge if you cover another classroom during the year.

▶ Each time you see parents, share at least one bit of positive news about their child from the day—a new accomplishment, for example, or something clever that their child said, or simply the fact that their child enjoyed a particular project. Simple, positive comments such as "Hayden completed a 24-piece puzzle today," "Sophie was a great helper today at clean-up time," or "Xiu really likes playing with blocks—she seems to get a real sense of accomplishment from building a tower" show parents that you are paying careful attention to their children and that their children are thriving under your care.

▶ Be sure to discuss any behavioral or developmental concerns with parents immediately. Make sure you let your director know about any serious concerns first so that she isn't surprised if the parents contact her about the situation. For example, if you are concerned about a child who has not been sleeping well during nap time, this is an important issue to discuss directly with parents—perhaps there are things going on at home, such as an impending move or a new sibling, that is troubling the child, and a brief chat with the parents can often give you the information you need to help deal with the problem. On the other hand, if one child has taken to biting other children and has just seriously bitten another child, make sure your director is aware of the incident and *then* discuss it calmly with the parents of both the biter and his victim. Your director will need to be aware of what happened in case the parents want to talk about the injury; besides, your director may have good advice about how to handle the child who is biting, especially if she knows that child well.

▶ Make sure you carefully document any problems you discuss with parents and any information you learn about the child or the family situation. If your center doesn't keep written records of this sort, keep your own notebook. That way you will always have documentation to refer back to should there be any future need.

Parent Involvement

Many preschools, childcare centers, and before- and after-school programs encourage—and, if they are cooperative centers, *require*—parents to participate in the program as classroom aides, chaperones, or as members of curriculum development, fundraising, or other committees. For example, parents of children enrolled at Weekday Nursery School, a cooperative preschool in South Orange, New Jersey, spend one morning each month serving as a teacher's helper, supervising children during art projects and other learning activities. This type of involvement offers another terrific opportunity to develop your relationship with parents and gain further insight into the children in your care.

UNDER A WATCHFUL EYE

As an early childhood educator, you will often be working on a team, sharing the responsibility of supervising children with others. In a larger center, for example, you may have a head teacher, coteacher, or assistant teacher with you all day in your classroom, while in a small center or homecare you may share the supervision of all the children with the director.

You may find it disconcerting to have colleagues constantly by your side, and you may feel like you are always being observed. Instead of feeling like Big Brother is watching, however, you should take comfort. If someone is in the room with you at all times, or most of the time, you have someone who can help you in a crisis and someone who can offer you feedback and advice informally and as difficult situations arise. For example, an assistant teacher can help you diffuse a conflict between two toddlers by distracting one child while you deal with the other. On the other hand, a more experienced head teacher can give you pointers on how to get a cranky child to cooperate.

Formal Observations

Formal observations may take place in your center or school on a regular basis, usually once or twice a year but sometimes more for first-year teachers. Of course, your director or supervisor may pop in for informal visits at any time. During these visits—whether they are formal or informal—it is important to *be yourself*. Don't try to impress; you will only create stress for yourself, and the children in your care will sense it immediately if you are nervous or tense. That may make *them* nervous and tense, too, and therefore less comfortable and less willing to cooperate. The more naturally you behave, and the more you stick to routine, the more likely your observation will go smoothly. Besides, if you are not yourself, how can you get honest, constructive feedback on your childcare techniques?

Strategies for Successful Coteaching

If you share teaching responsibility with another colleague, it is very important to establish a good relationship from the start. Once again, *communication is the key*. Be sure you are clear about who has what responsibilities, especially if one of you is of higher rank than the other. A head teacher, for example, may be responsible for planning the curriculum and documenting daily notes on child development while an assistant teacher may not have any curriculum development or documentation responsibilities. If you are coteachers on an equal level, be sure you share responsibilities in a way that makes you both comfortable. Do you want to divide duties equally? Switch tasks week to week? Discuss your strengths and weaknesses as well as your preferences with your colleague; decide who should handle which tasks and reevaluate your division of responsibilities regularly. Make important decisions, such as how to arrange the classroom, together. Regularly share information about children and their parents and discuss your concerns.

Of course, this is easier said than done; it is hard not to be nervous when you are being evaluated, especially if it is your first job. You are more likely to be relaxed if you have adapted well to the school culture, if you know and follow school philosophy and policies, and if you know exactly what to expect from your observation.

What the Observer Is Looking For

When your supervisor comes to observe you working with the children in your care, there are a few key things he or she will be looking for:

1. your ability to engage the children in meaningful, age-appropriate activities
2. your ability to stimulate the children's social, intellectual, and physical development
3. your ability to effectively manage the classroom

More specifically, the observer may be looking for the following qualities:

▶ What is your attitude toward your job? Do you seem to enjoy what you are doing, or do you seem to look upon your childcare tasks as a chore?

▶ What tone or manner do you use with the children? Are your comments age appropriate?

▶ Do you play favorites, or do you give all children equal attention?

▶ Are you flexible? Can you shift gears in the middle of a project or lesson in order to deal with a problem? If you want to talk about seasons, for example, but the children keep talking about the dead squirrel they saw in the playground, can you address their concerns and then gently guide the discussion back to your topic?

▶ Do you choose age-appropriate projects and activities that stimulate intellectual, social, and/or physical development? Are your lessons and activities creative and engaging?

▶ Do you encourage students and allow them to figure out solutions to problems on their own, or do you solve the problems for them?

▶ How do you handle conflicts between children?

▶ What do you do when a child will not cooperate?

▶ How do you comfort crying children?

▶ How comfortable do the children seem coming to you, or when you approach them?

▶ Is there evidence of learning and developmental growth among the children?

▶ Are you aware of potential dangers to children? Do you take steps to ensure their safety?

▶ Are you able to anticipate problems or conflicts between children and diffuse potential conflicts before they happen?

▶ Is the room neat and clean—or at least an "organized mess?"

▶ Do you shift instructional modes to meet the individual needs of the children?

MANAGING THE CHILDREN IN YOUR CARE

Even if you have already spent several years supervising children, you are bound to face many challenges working with a group of infants, toddlers, or preschoolers in a new environment. Now you will be responsible for a room full of children at approximately the same age and level of development—all of whom will need your attention, and all of whom have unique personalities and issues. How do you manage so many children at once?

Perhaps more important to your success as an early childhood educator than anything else is your ability to manage your classroom. With so many demands, such small children, and such short attention spans, how do you get things done in an organized and efficient manner? How do you get everyone to pay attention during story time or get cooperation when it is time to put away toys or clean up after lunch? How do you give everyone the attention and guidance they need throughout the day?

Average Childcare Worker to Child Ratio as Required by State Law

Age	Teacher:Child Ratio
Newborn–1 year	1:3 or 1:4
1–2 years	1:5
Preschool (2–5 years)	1:10

Source: Bureau of Labor Statistics *Occupational Outlook Handbook*, 2002–2003.

Being in charge of half a dozen energetic, exploring toddlers doesn't mean you have to feel like the old woman in the shoe who "had so many children she didn't know what to do." A few simple but important strategies can help you manage your classroom effectively.

Establish and Stick to Routine

Children will feel much more comfortable and be much more likely to cooperate if they know what is expected of them and if those expectations are consistent. Set a pattern for each day so that the children can expect a particular
routine each time they are in your care. For example, you may start each day
with free play, and then have clean-up time followed by a story. Then, you
might have a snack, followed again by clean-up, then arts and crafts followed
by lunch. A regular routine will help children get comfortable shifting gears.
And, when unexpected events interrupt your routine—as they inevitably will
do—you can use your structure to help children settle down and get the day
back on track.

Be Flexible

While it is important to establish and stick to routine as much as possible, it
is equally important to be flexible. With children, no amount of preparation
will ensure that things will go as planned. Always expect the unexpected to
interrupt your plans—and don't be ruffled when it does. If you don't get to
finish your counting lesson, for example, because two of the children had toi-
let accidents and a third has fallen and cut her knee, so be it; you can incor-
porate counting in your activities throughout the afternoon and/or finish the
lesson tomorrow.

Plan Your Lessons and Classroom Environment Carefully

You can minimize chaos and maximize learning by arranging your room
wisely. Set up separate areas for noisy and quiet play and use the furniture to
help divide the room into sections. Make sure activities are easy to access and
clean up, and decorate the room with pictures or other decorations that stimulate creativity and learning. And plan each day carefully. Prepare activities
that reinforce concepts the children are learning and give attention to different aspects of children's developmental needs. The more carefully (and
realistically) you plan, the easier it will be to handle the inevitable disruptions

and then get back on track. While flexibility is essential, "winging it" day to day will often leave you—and the children—frustrated and unhappy.

Be Realistic in Your Expectations

Remember the developmental level of the child and react appropriately. Even if you are caring for the "big kids" in the school, they are still very young, and if there are major events in their lives, such as potty training or the birth of a sibling, they are likely to regress in some areas. (It is a good idea to communicate with parents to keep up-to-date on these major events.) Remember what expectations and activities are appropriate for the children in your care. If a four-year-old is acting up, it could simply be that she is bored with a task that is too easy for her. Likewise, an angry two-year-old may be frustrated by the puzzle you have given him because it is too difficult; with a more age-appropriate task, he is much more likely to be both stimulated and content.

Stay Positive and Calm

Remember, your moods and feelings are contagious. If you overreact to minor incidents, you can expect the children in your care to overreact, too. If you remain calm—whether it is a hair-pulling fight or a major injury—you will do a much better job managing the situation and model good crisis management for the children and your colleagues. And keep a positive attitude. Your optimism will encourage the children to overcome obstacles and help them develop a healthy sense of independence and self-confidence.

Really Get to Know the Children in Your Care

The better you know the children in your classroom, the better you can guide their social, intellectual, and physical development. Observe them carefully and take note of their individual likes and dislikes; get familiar with their distinct rhythms. One five year old, for example, may still need quiet time in the afternoon, even though the other children don't nap; another may be easily frustrated and need extra encouragement when tackling new tasks. As Amy Quigley, a teacher of four year olds at Noah's Ark preschool in West Hartford, Connecticut, explains: "If you know their temperaments, you will be prepared for outbursts, likes and dislikes, when they need time to 'let loose,' and when they need quiet activities."

This kind of familiarity with the children in your care has other benefits, too: you get the unbeatable reward of watching the children accomplish goals and develop new skills. "Once you really get to know a child," says Quigley, "it is fascinating to watch them discover and develop new skills, vocabularies, and social interactions. For example, this is the second year I have had Mark in my class—he has a fall birthday and just turned five. Last year, he always wanted to play at the blocks and housekeeping centers; he would build these elaborate structures for dinosaurs, his favorite toy. He never chose the art/writing center. This year he is really into writing his name and drawing these amazing pictures of people, animals, and 'things,' and he really concentrates on what he is creating. He still likes to use his imagination in the block and housekeeping centers, but it is really interesting to see how he has developed more interest and skills in the art/writing center."

GETTING AHEAD: PROMOTIONS AND PROFESSIONAL DEVELOPMENT

Though opportunities for advancement may seem more limited for early childhood educators than for those working in large corporations, there are many ways to further your career as a caretaker of young children. As you gain experience and extend your training, you can move up the ranks, from assistant teacher to teacher, for example, or head teacher to curriculum developer or another supervisory position. Experience and additional education can also allow you to move into different types of schools or centers. For example, if you have an associate degree, you will be eligible to work in many types of daycare centers and preschools. However, without a bachelor's degree, you will not be able to work as a preschool teacher in most public school systems. And as you broaden your experience and education, you are more likely to succeed if you decide to open up your own homecare or preschool.

Continuing Education and Professional Development

Teaching is a profession where learning never stops. Even if you never take another formal class, as long as you care for children, you are still a student, always learning how to teach more effectively. Watching a child grow emotionally and intellectually is a wonderful experience, especially if you are contributing to that growth. Beyond this rewarding growth, as an early childhood educator, you will often be *required* to show proof of professional development in order to maintain or renew state licenses or get promotions; professional development for early childhood education is considered an ongoing process of refining skills and revising teaching methods. Because the early years in a child's life are so critical for development, it is especially important for caretakers to stay informed about the latest research in and philosophies about early childhood education.

Recent research suggests that professional development builds self-confidence in teachers and increases overall job satisfaction, making it an important benefit to both children and their caretakers. Professional development activities can take many forms, but generally, should fulfill the needs of the teacher and the goals of the school or center. In addition, professional development activities usually give caretakers an opportunity to meet new colleagues who can help broaden the knowledge and expertise needed to guide children.

Requirements for continuing education and professional development vary from state to state and from workplace to workplace and will also depend upon the certificate(s), degree(s) and/or license(s) you currently hold. Most states require proof that you have completed a given number of hours of professional development in order to renew your certification or license and will specify the eligible ways to accumulate those hours. Some states, including Vermont and New Jersey, may also require you to come up with an individual professional improvement plan and show evidence that you are taking steps toward your professional goals.

Types of Professional Development Activities

Anything from taking a college course in child psychology, to being on a curriculum development committee, or attending a workshop on nutrition may count toward fulfilling your professional development requirements. Here is a more detailed list of professional development activities for early childhood educators:

- ▶ formal, credit-bearing courses held at colleges and universities or online
- ▶ conferences, workshops, and seminars sponsored by colleges and universities, district boards of education, and professional associations
- ▶ courses, seminars, or other activities which are required for maintenance of licenses, or certificates issued by professional organizations or by your state government
- ▶ curriculum development (including research, writing, and revision)
- ▶ grant writing
- ▶ mentoring a novice teacher
- ▶ professional service on boards or committees
- ▶ developing and/or teaching a course or workshop
- ▶ contributions to professional literature, such as articles for early childhood education journals.

Be sure to check your state's certification and licensing requirements so you can choose the activities that will both further career goals and meet those requirements.

Where to Find Professional Development Activities

As you can see, there are many options for continuing education and professional development. If you are unclear about which professional development activities are best for your career goals, you can turn to a local professional organization for help. Connecticut, for example, has an excellent program for professional development in early childhood education called Connecticut-Charts-A-Course (www.ctcharts-a-course.org). Charts-A-Course members can receive career counseling and training. In addition, all Connecticut child-care providers who earn an income working directly with young children can apply for scholarship assistance from the organization in order to get certified and take courses that count toward virtually every degree.

If your state doesn't have a similar program, you can find plenty of opportunities for professional development through local chapters of national professional organizations, such as the National Association for the Education of Young Children (NAEYC). Local and regional chapters of the NAEYC offer conferences and workshops on various themes, such as the "United for Children" conference on discipline held in March 2002 in Houston, Texas, sponsored by the Houston Area Association for the Education of Young Children. Conference attendees listened to lectures by renowned experts and attended seminars and workshops devoted to issues in and research on discipline in the early childhood classroom. You can also contact local colleges and universities for appropriate courses in education, psychology, and business/management training.

TECHNOLOGY IN THE PRESCHOOL

Mira Sands of Atlanta, Georgia, is amazed by how much technology her four-year-old son Angelo understands. "He knows more about computers than I do!" she reports. "And he learned it in just a few weeks at daycare." Even children as young as 18 months are using computers at home and at school, learning and exploring through educational computer games and child-friendly sites on the Internet.

In fact, there is a tremendous range of computer games available to children, and many are of high educational value. *Dr. Seuss Toddler*, for example, for ages 18 months to three years, includes several activities that teach letter recognition, counting, number recognition, shapes, matching, and colors using colorful characters familiar to children. Good computer games fascinate children and teach a wide variety of concepts and skills, including:

▶ hand-eye coordination
▶ listening skills
▶ language skills
▶ number skills
▶ cause and effect

Even toddlers who aren't able to manipulate a mouse can begin developing these skills using special consoles that snap on top of regular keyboards.

While computer literacy may not be an official job requirement for most early childhood educators, it may soon be, and many centers are jumping on the technology bandwagon, creating "computer corners" or more elaborate computer centers and offering formal or informal technology instruction. In fact, some parents are only interested in preschools that include a introduction to computer skills for their children.

You have probably become comfortable with computers through your recent schooling, but if you are not yet computer literate, it is in your best interest to take some classes or find a tutor and learn the basics, even if you don't plan on getting your own personal computer. At a minimum, you should know how the key hardware components work together, how to open programs, and how to insert disks and CD-ROMs. Get comfortable with a mouse and learn how to browse the Internet. Check out websites for preschoolers, such as www.pbskids.org and http://disney.go.com, so that you can work with children comfortably in a familiar online environment.

CHALLENGES FOR EARLY CHILDHOOD EDUCATORS

As an early childhood educator, you will face many of the same challenges that teachers of all ages across the country face, such as long hours and low pay. But because you are dealing with such young children at such an important developmental age, you will also face special challenges and responsibilities and reap the unique rewards of helping to establish the foundation upon which their future learning will be based.

Emotional Involvement and Attachment

Unlike secondary school teachers, as an early childhood educator, you will be responsible for children who are highly dependent upon you for many of their physical and emotional needs. One of the joys of being a childcare worker is watching children develop a sense of independence, but be prepared for children to *need* you—and for you to become emotionally attached to some of the children.

You may also find yourself deeply involved in the lives of some of the children you care for and frustrated by family situations that you cannot change. Jennifer Simpson, for example, spent several years teaching in a public school with a pre-kindergarten program serving at-risk, inner city children in

Nashville, Tennessee. "There were several parents over the years who would smell of alcohol every day when they came to pick up their children," she recalls. "And then there was Anton. Parents from the neighborhood warned us that we were getting the worst kid from the projects that year—but we couldn't figure out who they were talking about. They meant Anton, but he turned out to be the best child in our class. He was four years old and raising his two-year-old brother because his mother and grandmother were both in and out of jail. He kept getting bounced around among family members but he would get himself up on his own and come to school every day. He took that responsibility on himself since no one else did. There was nothing we could do except give him as much love and support as we could while he was in our school."

But that love and support can make all the difference for an at-risk child. Later, when Anton was in third grade and back at Simpson's school, he wrote an entry in his journal about his preschool experience. "He wrote about how much he remembered preschool and how important it was to him. He loved it so much that he said he wanted to come to our classroom and help out, to help make a difference for other kids. It was really rewarding for us to see how much of a difference we had made in his life, even when we felt like our hands were tied."

Long Hours

Most early childhood education centers offer long hours, opening early so parents can drop off children before work and staying open late so parents can finish their work day before picking up their children. Centers open from 7:30 A.M. to 7:30 P.M., for example, often stagger shifts so employees don't have to work a 12-hour day, but you will often be expected to work long hours. An 8:30–5:30 day, for example, is not unusual, and if children have trouble during nap time, you may not even get a real break during the day. As an early childhood educator, you will need to have lots of energy to handle these hours, during which you will be running after children, stooping and bending to pick up children and toys, and cleaning up messes. Be prepared for your work to be physically exhausting sometimes.

Compensation

Educators across the nation are notoriously low-paid and, sadly, salaries for early childhood educators come in at the bottom of the scale. Despite the profound importance of intellectual and social development during the formative early childhood years, early childhood educators earned a median hourly income of just $7.43 in 2000, and the average annual salary for assistant teachers was only $17,350*. The government's Bureau of Labor Statistics also cites the following median hourly wages for childcare workers in 2000:

Residential care (nannies and home care providers)	$8.71/hour
Elementary schools	$8.52
Civic and social associations	$6.98
Child daycare services	$6.74
Miscellaneous amusement and recreation services	$6.65

*Source: Bureau of Labor Statistics *Occupational Outlook Handbook 2002–2003 Edition*
(http://www.bls.gov/oco/ocos170.htm)

Benefits, too, are often less comprehensive and generous for early childhood educators than for those in other careers, though there are often other payoffs. Preschool teachers working in elementary schools, for example, may be able to schedule vacation or personal days only if they coincide with school holidays, but they have up to two months off every summer. And while nannies typically do not receive any healthcare coverage from their employers, they do earn, on average, considerably more than other childcare workers. According to the International Nanny Association's (INA) 2001 Survey of Salaries and Benefits (available at www.nanny.org), the average gross hourly wage for nannies in 2001 was $10.25 per hour, and 95% of those surveyed reported receiving paid vacations of an average of two weeks. Fifty percent also said that employers contributed to healthcare costs, with contributions ranging from $50–$369 per month.

Finding your own healthcare coverage can be very expensive. The INA refers nannies to Eisenberg Associates (1-800-777-5765), a healthcare provider for independent childcare workers, and other health maintenance organizations such as US Healthcare offer coverage for individuals. But fees for individual coverage through health maintenance organizations can range from $200–$500 per month while family coverage typically begins at no less than $500 per month.

As Quigley and her colleagues point out, early childhood isn't a career you enter for the money—it's a career for those who truly love to work with children.

Lack of Respect

The low compensation for early childhood educators is in part a reflection of the overall lack of respect in which early childhood education is undeservedly held in our country. Early childhood educators receive special training and have a unique gift for caring for and guiding the social, intellectual, and physical growth of children, yet early childhood educators are often viewed as mere "babysitters" and many hold the view that caring for young children is an easy task. As a result, some parents and others in society assume that just about anyone can handle early childhood education tasks, and that while their children's caretakers enjoy working with children, they don't have any special training or skills. Trends such as the growing number of nanny schools and the increasing number of certificates available in early childhood education are helping to combat this notion. Maintaining a high degree of professionalism in your dealings with parents and encouraging parent involvement can also help to earn you the respect you deserve.

High Turnover

In part because of these challenges, and in part because, as Quigley points out, some people get involved in early childhood education "because they think it is easy and it is an income while they are working towards another career." Early childhood education is a field with a high turnover. And because early childhood education is a field that attracts people who love children, many teachers leave the job after a few years to raise a family.

This high turnover means that some children may have several teachers in one year—and this creates a special challenge for dedicated early childhood education professionals. You may face a bit of a struggle trying to gain the trust of children who may have felt abandoned by previous teachers. At the same time, however, high turnover means more job opportunities for early childhood educators. As the *Occupational Outlook Handbook* points out, "High turnover should create good opportunities for childcare workers. . . . Qualified persons who are interested in this work should have little trouble finding and keeping a job."

REAPING THE REWARDS

Though these challenges should not be taken lightly and are not to be ignored, if you are in early childhood education for the right reasons—if you truly love to work with children—these obstacles will pale in comparison to the rich rewards you will receive as an early childhood educator. With your training and expertise, with your compassion and concern for the well being of children, you will make a difference in many lives, and you will see evidence of your influence day after day. When you hear a child count to ten for the first time; when you see the joy in a child's face as he learns to put his socks on all by himself; when you listen to a child tell you how much she missed you over the weekend; and when you see children excited about ideas and skills that *you* introduced—you will know that low pay and other challenges aside, early childhood education is the right career for you.

THE INSIDE TRACK

Who: Tracey Loller
What: Remedial Kindergarten Teacher
Where: Bethlehem, PA

INSIDER'S STORY

I teach remedial classes for kindergarten though the Read to Succeed grant in an inner-city public school. I provide one-on-one instruction during the school day and small-group instruction in after-school sessions. I enjoy giving these young people a head start in life. It's amazing how each child is a unique individual, learning and growing in his or her own special way. Every new day is a challenge. Each student (especially in kindergarten) is at his or her own level of development—trying to meet each child's individual needs while encouraging them to grow a little further is very hard task. I feel the goal of every teacher should be to encourage independent learning, and when you see this occur it can be very rewarding.

I began teaching when my own children were school-aged. I think that being a parent gives you an entirely different perspective on parent-child relationships and child development. Sometimes, being a parent myself makes it even more frustrating when I deal with parents who don't have the same standards for their children as I do. It saddens me that a child can bring home something they made, or did well in, and he won't get praised for it at home. Apathy among many students is a big problem in our school.

Working with other teachers can also be challenging. The majority of teachers are neat people who really care about others, and I am shocked by the few who really don't seem to have the students' best interests at heart. I've encountered a few who really like to keep their ideas to themselves and like to keep their classroom in a little bubble. I feel that for a school to be successful you have to have to work cohesively toward the same goals. That said, most teachers are very willing to share what works for them and what doesn't.

Most of my job is very rewarding. In one of my classes, the teacher offered them an ice cream party when everyone learned the letters of their first name. This task can be especially difficult for our students who are bilingual. I had about ten students who took two weeks to master their name. The smile on their faces when they finally got it was a great feeling for everyone involved. We had one student who took particularly long to learn his name—it was wonderful to see the other children cheer for him when he finally got it. I don't believe their motive was solely the ice cream party, I think they were happy because most of them had gone through the struggle, too. They all patted him on the back and said, "Good job!" That was a great moment where he felt good about himself.

It's also wonderful to see a student who speaks little English and is quiet and withdrawn blossom. I have encountered quite a few students who suddenly stop following rules—they talk during story time or another listening activity. When this happened for the first time, the classroom teacher told me, "I know it's frustrating but that means your doing a good job. They are feeling confident enough to show their independence, just be consistent, firm, and understanding."

All in all, when you are working with young children, the most important quality to possess is patience. Teaching your young wards the basic skills they will need to succeed in life can be challenging in so many ways, you just have to wait, watch, and trust that what you are teaching them will sink in so that eventually they will become successful adults.

Appendix A

Professional Associations

A PROFESSIONAL association can be a valuable source of information, contacts, and opportunities for networking with others in the field, as well as discussions on the latest education philosophies and public policy. Through professional organizations you can find out about conferences, recent research, professional development classes, debates and resources. You can also work toward changing the current status of the profession, of children, or an aspect of childcare policy. You can even get the training you need, whether it is just a short course to help you manage your class or start your own daycare, or a course you want to take to better serve the children you teach. Professionals who are dedicated to the field are expected to show interest in the profession by being a part of a professional organization. Here are some organizations worth looking into.

American Montessori International/USA
410 Alexander Street
Rochester, NY 14607-1028
800-872-2643
Fax: 716-461-0075
www.montessori-ami.org

The AMI aims to further the study, application, and propagation of the Montessori ideals and principles for education and human development. The website lists accrediting centers where one may be trained according to the principles and practices of Montessori.

Association for Childhood Education International
17904 Georgia Avenue, Suite 215
Olney, MD 20832
800-423-3563
Fax: 301-570-2212
www.udel.edu/bateman/acei

The goal of the Association is to promote and support the optimal education and development of children from birth through early adolescence and to influence the professional growth of educators and the efforts of others committed to the needs of children in a changing society.

The Center for Early Childhood Leadership at National-Louis University

National-Louis University
6310 Capitol Drive
Wheeling, IL 60090
800-443-5522 ext. 7703
www.nl.edu/cecl

The Center for Early Childhood Leadership is dedicated to enhancing the management skills, professional orientation, and leadership capacity of early childhood administrators. The activities of the Center encompass four areas: training, technical assistance, research, and public awareness.

Center for the Child Care Workforce

733 15th Street NW, Suite 1037
Washington, DC 20005-2112
800-U-R-Worthy
Fax: 202-737-0370
www.ccw.org

The mission of the Center is to assure high quality, affordable childcare services by upgrading the training and compensation of teachers and childcare providers. The mission includes policy and program development, research and evaluation, and public education activities at the national, state, and local levels. The Center for the Child Care Workforce is working to bring fair wages to those who provide care for children.

Child Care Institute of America

3612 Bent Branch Court
Falls Church, VA 22041
703-941-4329
www.nccic.org/orgs/ccia.html

A national, non-profit organization that supports private-licensed, center based, and ecumenical early childhood programs.

The Council for Exceptional Children

1110 North Glebe Road, Suite 300
Arlington, VA 22201-5704
888-CEC-SPED
Fax: 703-264-9494
www.cec.sped.org

The Council for Exceptional Children (CEC) is the largest international professional organization dedicated to improving educational outcomes for individuals with exceptionalities, students with disabilities, and/or the gifted. The CEC advocates for appropriate governmental policies, sets professional standards, provides continual professional development, advocates for newly and historically underserved individuals with exceptionalities, and helps professionals obtain conditions and resources necessary for effective professional practice.

Council for Professional Recognition

2460 16th Street NW
Washington, DC 20009-3575
800-424-4310 or 202-265-9090
Fax: 202-265-9161
www.cdacouncil.org

The mission of the Council, a nonprofit corporation in Washington, DC, is to increase the status and recognition of early care and education professionals who care for children from birth through five years of age. Training teams conduct workshops for early childhood educators across the country, and members receive certification and ongoing professional development and advocacy opportunities.

International Nanny Association

900 Haddon Avenue, Suite 438
Collingswood, NJ 08108
856-858-0808
Fax: 856-858-2519
www.nanny.org

A non-profit association dedicated to providing education and support for nannies.

National Association of Child Care Professionals
P.O. Box 90723
Austin, TX 78709-0723
512-301-5557 or 800-537-1118
Fax: 512-301-5080
www.naccp.org

NACCP members are childcare owners, directors, and administrators from all kinds of childcare centers, regardless of tax status or corporate sponsorship. The organization's mission is to support those who lead the childcare industry.

National Association for the Education of Young Children (NAEYC)
1509 16th Street, N.W.
Washington, DC 20036-1426
202-232-8777 or 800-424-2460
Fax: 202-328-1846
www.naeyc.org

The nation's largest and most influential organization of early childhood educators and others is dedicated to improving the quality of programs for children from birth through third grade. NAEYC affiliate groups work to improve professional practice and working conditions in early childhood education and to build public support for high quality early childhood programs.

National Association of Child Care Resource and Referral Agencies (NACCRRA)
1319 F Street NW
Suite 500
Washington, DC 20004-1106
202-393-5501
Fax: 202-393-1109
www.naccrra.net

Dedicated to providing information to parents seeking childcare, childcare professionals, NACCRRA members, and childcare advocates. NACCRRA offers services to early childhood professionals and public policy makers, including: an Annual Policy Symposium, a list of publications and Technical Assistance Papers (TAPs), Internet-based resource and referral software, and online training.

National Association of Early Childhood Specialists in State Departments of Education
http://ericps.crc.uiuc.edu/naecs

A national organization for state education agency staff members with major responsibilities in the field of early childhood education. The Association promotes quality services to young children and their families through improvement of instruction, curriculum, and administration of programs.

National Association of Early Childhood Teacher Educators
www.naecte.org

An organization for teachers of early childhood education. Members receive opportunities for professional development, exchange ideas and discuss issues, and work toward improvements in early childhood teacher education. View the website to find your state affiliate's contact information.

National Association of Nannies
PMB 2004
25 Route 31 South, Suite-C
Pennington, NJ 08534-2511
800-344-6266
www.nannyassociation.com

The National Association of Nannies aims to promote the nanny profession, educating both nannies and the public about quality nanny care.

National Black Child Development Institute
1101 15th Street NW, Suite 900
Washington D.C. 20005
202-833-2220
www.nbcdi.org

The National Black Child Development Institute's African American Early Childhood Resource Center works to improve the quality of early care and education through leadership diversity. The Resource Center is a clearinghouse for enhancing the diversity of ECE leadership and improving the quality of ECE practices.

National Child Care Association
1016 Rosser Street
Conyers, GA 30012
800-543-7161
www.nccanet.org

The National Child Care Association's mission is to promote the growth and interests of early childhood educators. The organization's efforts focus on assisting licensed, private childcare providers.

National Head Start Association
1651 Prince Street
Alexandria, VA 22314
703-739-0875
Fax: 703-739-0878
www.nhsa.org

The National Head Start Association (NHSA) is a private, not-for-profit membership organization representing more than 2,400 Head Start programs in America. NHSA provides a national forum for the continued enhancement of Head Start services for poor children up to five years of age, and their families.

National Institute on Early Childhood Development and Education
555 New Jersey Avenue NW
Washington, DC 20208
202-219-1935
Fax: 202-273-4768
www.ed.gov/offices/OERI/ECI/index.html

The National Institute on Early Childhood Development and Education (ECI) was created to carry out a comprehensive program of research, development, and dissemination to improve early childhood development and learning.

National Organization of Child Development Laboratory Schools
http://cdl.uiuc.edu/nocdls/nocdls.html

The NOCDLS was created in order to support and encourage a network system among professionals working in lab schools on college and university campuses.

Quilt: Quality in Linking Together: Early Education Partnerships
877-TO-QUILT
www.quilt.org

Quality in Linking Together Early Education Partnerships (QUILT) is a national training and technical assistance project funded by the Federal Head Start and Child Care Bureaus. Its purpose is to support full-day, full-year partnerships among child care, Head Start, pre-kindergarten, and other early education programs at the local, state, tribal, territorial, and regional levels.

Southern Early Childhood Association
1-800-305-7322
Fax: 501-227-5297
www.seca50.org

The Association brings together preschool, kindergarten and primary teachers, administrators, caregivers, program directors, and individuals working with and for families to promote quality care and education for young children. Members share ideas in local, state and regional meetings, in professional development institutes, and through the association's publications and resources.

USA Child Care
703-938-5531
Fax: 703-255-6859
www.usachildcare.org

The organization supports child care providers who are committed to serving children from low- and moderate-income families. Its mission is to bring the voice of direct services providers to national and state policy dialogue.

U.S. National Committee of the World Organization for Early Childhood Education
Dr. Cathy Mogharreban, Treasurer OMEP-USNC
Dept. of Curriculum and Instruction MC 4610
Southern Illinois University
Carbondale, IL 62901-4610
http://omep-usnc.org

OMEP's objective is to promote the optimum conditions for the well-being of all children, their development and happiness within their families, institutions, and society. To this end, OMEP assists any undertaking to improve early childhood education, and supports scientific research that can influence these conditions.

Zero to Three: National Center for Infants, Toddlers and Families
2000 M Street NW, Suite 200
Washington, D.C. 20036
202-638-1144
Fax: 202-638-0851
www.zerotothree.org

Zero to Three is a national non-profit charitable organization whose aim is to strengthen and support families, practitioners, and communities to promote the healthy development of babies and toddlers. The organization disseminates developmental information, trains providers, promotes model approaches and standards of practice, and works to increase public awareness about the significance of the first three years of life.

Appendix B

Additional Resources for Teachers

THE FOLLOWING directory provides information that could be useful to early childhood educators online and in print.

ONLINE RESOURCES

Head Start Bureau
330 C Street, SW
Washington, DC 20447
202-205-8572
www.acf.dhhs.gov/programs/hsb

Head Start is a child development program that serves low-income children and their families. The Head Start Bureau maintains this web site as an electronic resource for Head Start service providers, parents, volunteers, community organizations, and others.

National Child Care Information Center
243 Church Street, NW, 2nd Floor
Vienna, VA 22180
800-616-2242
Fax: 800-716-2242
www.nccic.org

This national resource links information and people to complement, enhance, and promote the childcare delivery system, working to ensure that all children and families have access to high-quality services.

National Information Center for Children and Youth with Disabilities
P.O. Box 1492
Washington, DC 20013
800-695-0285
www.nichcy.org

This is a national referral center that provides information on disabilities and disability-related issues for families, educators, and other professionals.

National Resource Center for Health and Safety in Child Care
UCHSC at Fitzsimons
National Resource Center for Health and
    Safety in Child Care
Campus Mail Stop F541
P.O. Box 6508
Aurora, CO 80045-0508
Fax: 303-724-0960
http://nrc.uchsc.edu

The National Resource Center is located at the University of Colorado Health Sciences Center and is funded by the Maternal and Child Health Bureau, U.S. Department of Health & Human Services, HRSA. NRC's primary mission is to promote health and safety in out-of-home childcare settings throughout the nation.

ERIC
ACCESS ERIC
2277 Research Boulevard
MS 4M
Rockville, MD 20850
800-538-3742
www.eric.ed.gov

The Educational Resources Information Center (ERIC) is a national information system designed to provide ready access to education-related literature. ERIC is supported by the U.S. Department of Education. At the heart of ERIC is the education database, containing more than one million records of journal articles, research reports, curriculum and teaching guides, conference papers, and books.

Bureau of Labor Statistics
U.S. Bureau of Labor Statistics
Postal Square Building
2 Massachusetts Avenue NE
Washington, DC 20212-0001
202-691-5200
Fax: 202-691-6325
www.bls.gov

The Bureau of Labor Statistics is the principal fact-finding agency for the federal government. Here you can find the average wages for early childhood education general employment statistics on the local and national level, employment projections, and the *Occupational Outlook Handbook*, published by the agency.

Early Education Clearinghouse
95 Berkeley Street, Suite 306
Boston, MA 02116
617-695-0700 X271
Fax: 617-695-9590
www.factsinaction.org

The Early Education Clearinghouse works to put research-based knowledge and tools into the hands of those who serve in the early childhood field, as well as those who influence or make policy that affects the field. On this site, you can find summaries of recent research, important facts and statistics, reports on tools you can use to measure the outcomes of your work, and legislative and administrative policy updates. Each article focuses on findings and action steps you can take.

U.S. Department of Education
U.S. Department of Education
400 Maryland Avenue SW
Washington, DC 20202-0498
800-USA-LEARN (800-872-5327)
www.ed.gov

Here is a website for both students and teachers. If you are considering going to college or going back to school for an advanced degree, you will find information on programs and financial aid on this site. If you are a teacher already, this website will help you find out more about education policy, teaching incentives and programs, as well as government grants for teaching programs and research in education.

State Child Care Licensing Offices
http://ed.gov/Programs/bastmp/SCCLO.htm

This web page contains hypertext links or pointers to information created and maintained by different public and private organizations relevant to education.

The National Resource Center For Health and Safety in Child Care
http://nrc.uchsc.edu/states.html

This website contains childcare regulations for all of the states in one location. Check out the standards for your state.

BOOKS

Billman, Jean. *Observation and Participation in Early Childhood Settings: A Practicum Guide* (Boston, MA: Allyn & Bacon, 1995).

Boydston, Joel. *Teacher Certification Requirements in All Fifty States 2001-2002: How and Where to Get a Teaching Certificate in All Fifty States* (Sebring, FL: Teacher Certification Publications, 2001).

Brause, Rita et al. *Succeeding at Your Interview: A Practical Guide for Teachers* (Mahwah, NJ: Lawrence Erlbaum Assoc, 2001).

Cassidy, Daniel. *The Scholarship Book 2002* (Upper Saddle River, NJ: Prentice Hall Press, 2001).

Catlin, Cynthia. *Toddlers Together: The Complete Planning Guide for a Toddler Curriculum* (Beltsville, MD: Gryphon House, 1994).

Criscito, Pat. *Barron's Guide to Distance Learning: Degrees, Certificates, Courses* (Hauppauge, NY: Barron's Educational Series, 1999).

Eberts, Marjorie and Gisler, Margaret. *Careers in Child Care* (New York, NY: McGraw Hill, 2000).

Evans, Roy. *Teacher Preparation for Early Childhood Education* (New York, NY: Gordon & Breach Science Pub., 1993).

Gonzalez-Mena, Janet. *Foundation: Early Childhood Education in a Diverse Society* (New York, NY: Mayfield Publishing, 2000).

Herr, Judy et al. *Creative Resources for the Early Childhood Classroom* (Albany, NY: Delmar Publishers, 1999).

Isabell, Rebecca et al. *Early Learning Environments that Work* (Beltsville, MD: Gryphon House, 2001).

Lay-Dopyera, Margaret. *Becoming a Teacher of Young Children* (New York, NY: McGraw-Hill, 1992).

Lillard, Paula. *Montessori in the Classroom: A Teacher's Account of How Children Really Learn* (New York, NY: Schocken Books, 1997).

McKinney, Anne. *Real-Resumes for Teachers* (Fayetteville, NC: PREP Publishing, 2000).

Melenyzer, Beverly. *How to Develop a Professional Portfolio: A Manual for Teachers* (Boston, MA: Allyn & Bacon, 2000).

Petersen, Evelyn. *Practical Guide to Early Childhood Planning, Methods and Materials, A: The What, Why and How of Lesson Plans* (Boston, MA: Allyn & Bacon, 1995).

Rosenberg, Arthur and Hizer, David. *The Resume Handbook: How to Write Outstanding Resumes and Cover Letters for Every Situation* (Avon, MA: Adams Media Corporation, 1996).

The College Board College Cost & Financial Aid Handbook 2002 (NY: College Entrance Examination Board, 2002).

Weitzman, Elaine. *Learning Language and Loving It: A Guide for Promoting Children's Social and Language Development in Early Childhood Settings* (Toronto, Canada: The Hanen Centre, 1992).

Yate, Martin. *Cover Letters That Knock 'Em Dead* (Avon, MA: Adams Media Corporation, 2000).

Appendix C

Sample Free Application for Federal Student Aid (FAFSA)

ON THE following pages you will find a sample FAFSA. Use this opportunity to familiarize yourself with the form so that when you apply for federal and state student grants, work-study, and loans you will know what information you need to have ready. At print this was the most current form, and although the form remains mostly the same from year to year, you should check the FAFSA website (www.fafsa.ed.gov) for the most current information.

2001-2002

The FAFSA

July 1, 2001 — June 30, 2002
Free Application for Federal Student Aid

OMB # 1845-0001

Use this form to apply for federal and state* student grants, work-study, and loans.

Apply over the Internet with

FAFSA ON THE WEB   **www.fafsa.ed.gov**

If you are filing a **2000 income tax return,** we recommend that you complete it before filling out this form. However, you do not need to file your income tax return with the IRS before you submit this form.

If you or your family has **unusual circumstances** (such as loss of employment) that might affect your need for student financial aid, submit this form, and then consult with the financial aid office at the college you plan to attend.

You may also use this form to apply for **aid from other sources, such as your state or college.** The deadlines for states (see table to right) or colleges may be as early as January 2001 and may differ. You may be required to complete additional forms. Check with your high school guidance counselor or a financial aid administrator at your college about state and college sources of student aid.

Your answers on this form will be read electronically. Therefore:

- use black ink and fill in ovals completely:
- print clearly in CAPITAL letters and skip a box between words:
- report dollar amounts (such as $12,356.41) like this:

Yes ●   No ✕ ✓

| 1 | 5 | | E | L | M | | S | T |

$ | | 1 | 2 | , | 3 | 5 | 6 | **no cents**

Green is for students and purple is for parents.

If you have questions about this application, or for more information on eligibility requirements and the U.S. Department of Education's student aid programs, look on the Internet at **www.ed.gov/studentaid** You can also call 1-800-4FED-AID (1-800-433-3243) seven days a week from 8:00 a.m. through midnight (Eastern time). TTY users may call 1-800-730-8913.

After you complete this application, make a copy of it for your records. Then **send the original of pages 3 through 6** in the attached envelope or send it to: Federal Student Aid Programs, P.O. Box 4008, Mt. Vernon, IL 62864-8608.

You should submit your application as early as possible, but no earlier than January 1, 2001. We must receive your application **no later than July 1, 2002.** Your school must have your correct, complete information by your last day of enrollment in the 2001-2002 school year.

You should hear from us within four weeks. If you do not, please call 1-800-433-3243 or check on-line at www.fafsa.ed.gov

Now go to page 3 and begin filling out this form.
Refer to the notes as needed.

STATE AID DEADLINES

STATE AID DEADLINES

AR   April 1, 2001 *(date received)*
AZ   June 30, 2002 *(date received)*
*^ CA   March 2, 2001 *(date postmarked)*
* DC   June 24, 2001 *(date received by state)*
DE   April 15, 2001 *(date received)*
FL   May 15, 2001 *(date processed)*
HI   March 1, 2001
^ IA   July 1, 2001 *(date received)*
IL   First-time applicants – September 30, 2001
Continuing applicants – July 15, 2001
(date received)
^ IN   For priority consideration – March 1, 2001
(date postmarked)
* KS   For priority consideration – April 1, 2001
(date received)
KY   For priority consideration – March 15, 2001
(date received)
^ LA   For priority consideration – April 15, 2001
Final deadline – July 1, 2001
(date received)
^ MA   For priority consideration – May 1, 2001
(date received)
MD   March 1, 2001 *(date postmarked)*
ME   May 1, 2001 *(date received)*
MI   High school seniors – February 21, 2001
College students – March 21, 2001
(date received)
MN   June 30, 2002 *(date received)*
MO   April 1, 2001 *(date received)*
MT   For priority consideration – March 1, 2001
(date postmarked)
NC   March 15, 2001 *(date received)*
ND   April 15, 2001 *(date processed)*
NH   May 1, 2001 *(date received)*
^ NJ   June 1, 2001 if you received a
Tuition Aid Grant in 2000-2001
All other applicants
– October 1, 2001, for fall and spring terms
– March 1, 2002, for spring term only
(date received)
*^ NY   May 1, 2002 *(date postmarked)*
OH   October 1, 2001 *(date received)*
OK   For priority consideration – April 30, 2001
Final deadline – June 30, 2001
(date received)
OR   May 1, 2002 *(date received)*
* PA   All 2000-2001 State Grant recipients and all
non-2000-2001 State Grant recipients in
degree programs – May 1, 2001
All other applicants – August 1, 2001
(date received)
PR   May 2, 2002 *(date application signed)*
RI   March 1, 2001 *(date received)*
SC   June 30, 2001 *(date received)*
TN   May 1, 2001 *(date processed)*
*^ WV   March 1, 2001 *(date received)*

Check with your financial aid administrator for these states: AK, AL, *AS, *CT, CO, *FM, GA, *GU, ID, *MH, *MP, MS, *NE, *NM, *NV, *PW, *SD, *TX, UT, *VA, *VI, *VT, WA, WI, and *WY.

^ *Applicants encouraged to obtain proof of mailing.*
* *Additional form may be required*

Notes for questions 13-14 (page 3)

If you are an eligible noncitizen, write in your eight or nine digit Alien Registration Number. Generally, you are an eligible noncitizen if you are: (1) a U.S. permanent resident and you have an Alien Registration Receipt Card (I-551); (2) a conditional permanent resident (I-551C); or (3) an other eligible noncitizen with an Arrival-Departure Record (I-94) from the U.S. Immigration and Naturalization Service showing any one of the following designations: "Refugee," "Asylum Granted," "Indefinite Parole," "Humanitarian Parole," or "Cuban-Haitian Entrant." If you are in the U.S. on only an F1 or F2 student visa, or only a J1 or J2 exchange visitor visa, or a G series visa (pertaining to international organizations), you must fill in oval c. If you are neither a citizen nor eligible noncitizen, you are not eligible for federal student aid. However, you may be eligible for state or college aid.

Notes for questions 17-21 (page 3)

For undergraduates, full time generally means taking at least 12 credit hours in a term or 24 clock hours per week. 3/4 time generally means taking at least 9 credit hours in a term or 18 clock hours per week. Half time generally means taking at least 6 credit hours in a term or 12 clock hours per week. Provide this information about the college you plan to attend.

Notes for question 29 (page 3) — Enter the correct number in the box in question 29.

Enter **1** for 1ˢᵗ bachelor's degree
Enter **2** for 2ⁿᵈ bachelor's degree
Enter **3** for associate degree (occupational or technical program)
Enter **4** for associate degree (general education or transfer program)
Enter **5** for certificate or diploma for completing an occupational, technical, or educational program of less than two years
Enter **6** for certificate or diploma for completing an occupational, technical, or educational program of at least two years
Enter **7** for teaching credential program (nondegree program)
Enter **8** for graduate or professional degree
Enter **9** for other/undecided

Notes for question 30 (page 3) — Enter the correct number in the box in question 30.

Enter **0** for 1st year undergraduate/never attended college
Enter **1** for 1st year undergraduate/attended college before
Enter **2** for 2nd year undergraduate/sophomore
Enter **3** for 3rd year undergraduate/junior
Enter **4** for 4th year undergraduate/senior
Enter **5** for 5th year/other undergraduate
Enter **6** for 1st year graduate/professional
Enter **7** for continuing graduate/professional or beyond

Notes for questions 37 c. and d. (page 4) and 71 c. and d. (page 5)

If you filed or will file a foreign tax return, or a tax return with Puerto Rico, Guam, American Samoa, the Virgin Islands, the Marshall Islands, the Federated States of Micronesia, or Palau, use the information from that return to fill out this form. If you filed a foreign return, convert all figures to U.S. dollars, using the exchange rate that is in effect today.

Notes for questions 38 (page 4) and 72 (page 5)

In general, a person is eligible to file a 1040A or 1040EZ if he or she makes less than $50,000, does not itemize deductions, does not receive income from his or her own business or farm, and does not receive alimony. A person is not eligible if he or she itemizes deductions, receives self-employment income or alimony, or is required to file Schedule D for capital gains.

Notes for questions 41 (page 4) and 75 (page 5) — only for people who filed a 1040EZ or Telefile

On the 1040EZ, if a person answered "Yes" on line 5, use EZ worksheet line F to determine the number of exemptions ($2,800 equals one exemption). If a person answered "No" on line 5, enter 01 if he or she is single, or 02 if he or she is married.

On the Telefile, use line J to determine the number of exemptions ($2,800 equals one exemption).

Notes for questions 47-48 (page 4) and 81-82 (page 5)

Net worth means current value minus debt. If net worth is one million or more, enter $999,999. If net worth is negative, enter 0.

Investments include real estate (do not include the home you live in), trust funds, money market funds, mutual funds, certificates of deposit, stocks, stock options, bonds, other securities, education IRAs, installment and land sale contracts (including mortgages held), commodities, etc. Investment value includes the market value of these investments as of today. Investment debt means only those debts that are related to the investments.

Investments do not include the home you live in, cash, savings, checking accounts, the value of life insurance and retirement plans (pension funds, annuities, noneducation IRAs, Keogh plans, etc.), or the value of prepaid tuition plans.

Business and/or investment farm value includes the market value of land, buildings, machinery, equipment, inventory, etc. Business and/or investment farm debt means only those debts for which the business or investment farm was used as collateral.

Notes for question 58 (page 4)

Answer **"No"** (you are not a veteran) if you (1) have never engaged in active duty in the U.S. Armed Forces, (2) are currently an ROTC student or a cadet or midshipman at a service academy, or (3) are a National Guard or Reserves enlistee activated only for training. Also answer "No" if you are currently serving in the U.S. Armed Forces and will continue to serve through June 30, 2002.

Answer **"Yes"** (you are a veteran) if you (1) have engaged in active duty in the U.S. Armed Forces (Army, Navy, Air Force, Marines, or Coast Guard) or as a member of the National Guard or Reserves who was called to active duty for purposes other than training, or were a cadet or midshipman at one of the service academies, **and** (2) were released under a condition other than dishonorable. Also answer "Yes" if you are not a veteran now but will be one by June 30, 2002.

Step One: For questions 1-34, leave blank any questions that do not apply to you (the student).

1-3. Your full name (as it appears on your Social Security Card)

1. LAST NAME	2. FIRST NAME	3. MIDDLE INITIAL
FOR INFORMATION ONLY	DO NOT SUBMIT	

4-7. Your permanent mailing address

4. NUMBER AND STREET (INCLUDE APT. NUMBER)

5. CITY (AND COUNTRY IF NOT U.S.)   6. STATE   7. ZIP CODE

8. Your Social Security Number
XXX – XX – XXXX

9. Your date of birth
/ / 1 9

10. Your permanent telephone number
( ) –

11-12. Your driver's license number and state (if any)

11. LICENSE NUMBER   12. STATE

13. Are you a U.S. citizen? Pick one. **See Page 2.**
- a. Yes, I am a U.S. citizen. .... ○ 1
- b. No, but I am an eligible noncitizen. **Fill in question 14.** .... ○ 2
- c. No, I am not a citizen or eligible noncitizen. .... ○ 3

14. ALIEN REGISTRATION NUMBER
A

15. What is your marital status as of today?
- I am single, divorced, or widowed. ○ 1
- I am married/remarried. ○ 2
- I am separated. ○ 3

16. Month and year you were married, separated, divorced, or widowed
MONTH   YEAR
/

For each question (17 - 21), please mark whether you will be full time, 3/4 time, half time, less than half time, or not attending. **See page 2.**

		Full time/Not sure	3/4 time	Half time	Less than half time	Not attending
17.	Summer 2001	○ 1	○ 2	○ 3	○ 4	○ 5
18.	Fall 2001	○ 1	○ 2	○ 3	○ 4	○ 5
19.	Winter 2001-2002	○ 1	○ 2	○ 3	○ 4	○ 5
20.	Spring 2002	○ 1	○ 2	○ 3	○ 4	○ 5
21.	Summer 2002	○ 1	○ 2	○ 3	○ 4	○ 5

		Middle school/Jr. High	High school	College or beyond	Other/unknown
22.	Highest school your father completed	○ 1	○ 2	○ 3	○ 4
23.	Highest school your mother completed	○ 1	○ 2	○ 3	○ 4

24. What is your state of legal residence?
STATE

25. Did you become a legal resident of this state before January 1, 1996?
Yes ○ 1   No ○ 2

26. If the answer to question 25 is **"No,"** give month and year you became a legal resident.
MONTH   YEAR
/

27. Are you male? (Most male students must register with Selective Service to get federal aid.)
Yes ○ 1   No ○ 2

28. If you are male (age 18-25) and not registered, do you want Selective Service to register you?
Yes ○ 1   No ○ 2

29. What degree or certificate will you be working on during 2001-2002? **See page 2** and enter the correct number in the box.

30. What will be your grade level when you begin the 2001-2002 school year? **See page 2** and enter the correct number in the box.

31. Will you have a high school diploma or GED before you enroll?
Yes ○ 1   No ○ 2

32. Will you have your first bachelor's degree before July 1, 2001?
Yes ○ 1   No ○ 2

33. In addition to grants, are you interested in student loans (which you must pay back)?
Yes ○ 1   No ○ 2

34. In addition to grants, are you interested in "work-study" (which you earn through work)?
Yes ○ 1   No ○ 2

35. Do not leave this question blank. Have you ever been convicted of possessing or selling illegal drugs? If you have, answer "Yes," complete and submit this application, and we will send you a worksheet in the mail for you to determine if your conviction affects your eligibility for aid.
No ○ 1   Yes ○ 3

DO NOT LEAVE QUESTION 35 BLANK

Step Two:
For questions 36-49, report your (the student's) income and assets. If you are married, report your spouse's income and assets, even if you were not married in 2000. Ignore references to "spouse" if you are currently single, separated, divorced, or widowed.

36. For 2000, have you (the student) completed your IRS income tax return or another tax return listed in **question 37**?

a. I have already completed my return. ○ 1   **b.** I will file, but I have not yet ○ 2   **c.** I'm not going to file. **(Skip to question 42.)** ○ 3
completed my return.

37. What income tax return did you file or will you file for 2000?

a. IRS 1040 .... ○ 1   **d.** A tax return for Puerto Rico, Guam, American Samoa, the Virgin Islands, the
b. IRS 1040A, 1040EZ, 1040Telefile ...... ○ 2   Marshall Islands, the Federated States of Micronesia, or Palau. **See Page 2.** ...... ○ 4
c. A foreign tax return. **See Page 2.** ...... ○ 3

38. If you have filed or will file a 1040, were you eligible to file a 1040A or 1040EZ? **See page 2.**   Yes ○ 1   No ○ 2   Don't Know ○ 3

For questions 39-51, if the answer is zero or the question does not apply to you, enter 0.

39. What was your (and spouse's) adjusted gross income for 2000? Adjusted gross income is on IRS Form 1040–line 33; 1040A–line 19; 1040EZ–line 4; or Telefile–line I. $ [   ] , [   ]

40. Enter the total amount of your (and spouse's) income tax for 2000. Income tax amount is on IRS Form 1040–line 51; 1040A–line 33; 1040EZ–line 10; or Telefile–line K. $ [   ] , [   ]

41. Enter your (and spouse's) exemptions for 2000. Exemptions are on IRS Form 1040–line 6d or on Form 1040A–line 6d. For Form 1040EZ or Telefile, **see page 2.**   [   ]

42-43. How much did you (and spouse) earn from working in 2000? Answer this question whether or not you filed a tax return. This information may be on your W-2 forms, or on IRS Form 1040–lines 7 + 12 + 18; 1040A–line 7; or 1040EZ–line 1. Telefilers should use their W-2's.
You (42) $ [   ] , [   ]
Your Spouse (43) $ [   ] , [   ]

Student (and Spouse) Worksheets (44-46)

44-46. Go to Page 8 and complete the columns on the left of Worksheets A, B, and C. Enter the student (and spouse) totals in questions 44, 45, and 46, respectively. Even though you may have few of the Worksheet items, check each line carefully.
Worksheet A (44) $ [   ] , [   ]
Worksheet B (45) $ [   ] , [   ]
Worksheet C (46) $ [   ] , [   ]

47. As of today, what is the net worth of your (and spouse's) current **investments**? **See page 2.** $ [   ] , [   ]

48. As of today, what is the net worth of your (and spouse's) current **businesses and/or investment farms**? **See page 2.** Do not include a farm that you live on and operate. $ [   ] , [   ]

49. As of today, what is your (and spouse's) total current balance of cash, savings, and checking accounts? $ [   ] , [   ]

50-51. If you receive veterans education benefits, for **how many months** from July 1, 2001 through June 30, 2002 will you receive these benefits, and **what amount** will you receive per month? Do not include your spouse's veterans education benefits.
Months (50) [   ]
Amount (51) $ [   ]

Step Three:
Answer all seven questions in this step.

52. Were you born before January 1, 1978? ....   Yes ○ 1   No ○ 2

53. Will you be working on a master's or doctorate program (such as an MA, MBA, MD, JD, or Ph.D., etc.) during the school year 2001-2002? ....   Yes ○ 1   No ○ 2

54. As of today, are you married? (Answer "Yes" if you are separated but not divorced.) ....   Yes ○ 1   No ○ 2

55. Do you have children who receive more than half of their support from you? ....   Yes ○ 1   No ○ 2

56. Do you have dependents (other than your children or spouse) who live with you and who receive more than half of their support from you, now and through June 30, 2002? ....   Yes ○ 1   No ○ 2

57. Are you an orphan or ward of the court or were you a ward of the court until age 18? ....   Yes ○ 1   No ○ 2

58. Are you a veteran of the U.S. Armed Forces? **See page 2.** ....   Yes ○ 1   No ○ 2

If you (the student) answer "No" to every question in Step Three, go to Step Four.
If you answer "Yes" to any question in Step Three, skip Step Four and go to Step Five.

(If you are a graduate health profession student, your school may require you to complete Step Four even if you answered "Yes" in Step Three.)

Step Four: Complete this step if you (the student) answered "No" to all questions in Step Three.

59. Go to page 7 to determine who is considered a parent for this step. What is your parents' marital status as of today?

(Pick one.) Married/Remarried ○ 1 Single ○ 2 Divorced/Separated ○ 3 Widowed ○ 4

60-63. What are your parents' Social Security Numbers and last names?
If your parent does not have a Social Security Number, enter 000-00-0000

60. FATHER'S/STEPFATHER'S SOCIAL SECURITY NUMBER X X X – X X – X X X X

61. FATHER'S/STEPFATHER'S LAST NAME F O R I N F O R M A T I O N O N L Y

62. MOTHER'S/STEPMOTHER'S SOCIAL SECURITY NUMBER X X X – X X – X X X X

63. MOTHER'S/STEPMOTHER'S LAST NAME D O N O T S U B M I T

64. Go to page 7 to determine how many people are in your parents' household.

65. Go to page 7 to determine how many in question 64 **(exclude your parents)** will be college students between July 1, 2001 and June 30, 2002.

66. What is your parents' state of legal residence? | STATE

67. Did your parents become legal residents of the state in question 66 before January 1, 1996? | Yes ○ 1 No ○ 2

68. If the answer to question 67 is "No," give the month and year legal residency began for the parent who has lived in the state the longest. | MONTH YEAR | /

69. What is the age of your older parent?

70. For 2000, have your parents completed their IRS income tax return or another tax return listed in **question 71**?

a. My parents have already completed their return. ○ 1

b. My parents will file, but they have not yet completed their return. ○ 2

c. My parents are not going to file. **(Skip to question 76.)** ○ 3

71. What income tax return did your parents file or will they file for 2000?

a. IRS 1040 .... ○ 1

b. IRS 1040A, 1040EZ, 1040Telefile ..... ○ 2

c. A foreign tax return. **See Page 2.** ...... ○ 3

d. A tax return for Puerto Rico, Guam, American Samoa, the Virgin Islands, the Marshall Islands, the Federated States of Micronesia, or Palau. **See Page 2.** .... ○ 4

72. If your parents have filed or will file a 1040, were they eligible to file a 1040A or 1040EZ? **See page 2.** | Yes ○ 1 No ○ 2 Don't Know ○ 3

For questions 73 - 83, if the answer is zero or the question does not apply, enter 0.

73. What was your parents' adjusted gross income for 2000? Adjusted gross income is on IRS Form 1040–line 33; 1040A–line 19; 1040EZ–line 4; or Telefile–line I. | $,

74. Enter the total amount of your parents' income tax for 2000. Income tax amount is on IRS Form 1040–line 51; 1040A–line 33; 1040EZ–line 10; or Telefile–line K. | $,

75. Enter your parents' exemptions for 2000. Exemptions are on IRS Form 1040–line 6d or on Form 1040A–line 6d. For Form 1040EZ or Telefile, **see page 2.**

76-77. How much did your parents earn from working in 2000? Answer this question whether or not your parents filed a tax return. This information may be on their W-2 forms, or on IRS Form 1040–lines 7 + 12 + 18; 1040A–line 7; or 1040EZ–line 1. Telefilers should use their W-2's.

Father/ Stepfather (76) $,

Mother/ Stepmother (77) $,

Parent Worksheets (78-80)

78-80. Go to Page 8 and complete the columns on the right of Worksheets A, B, and C. Enter the parent totals in questions 78, 79, and 80, respectively. Even though your parents may have few of the Worksheet items, check each line carefully.

Worksheet A (78) $,

Worksheet B (79) $,

Worksheet C (80) $,

81. As of today, what is the net worth of your parents' current **investments**? **See page 2.** | $,

82. As of today, what is the net worth of your parents' current **businesses and/or investment farms**? **See page 2.** Do not include a farm that your parents live on and operate. | $,

83. As of today, what is your parents' total current balance of cash, savings, and checking accounts? | $,

Now go to Step Six.

For Help — (800) 433-3243

Step Five: Complete this step only if you (the student) answered "Yes" to any question in Step Three.

84. Go to page 7 to determine how many people are in your (and your spouse's) household. ☐☐

85. Go to page 7 to determine how many in question 84 will be college students between July 1, 2001 and June 30, 2002. ☐

Step Six: Please tell us which schools should receive your information.

For each school (up to six), please provide the federal school code and your housing plans. Look for the federal school codes on the Internet at **www.fafsa.ed.gov**, at your college financial aid office, at your public library, or by asking your high school guidance counselor. If you cannot get the federal school code, write in the complete name, address, city, and state of the college.

	1ST FEDERAL SCHOOL CODE		NAME OF COLLEGE / ADDRESS AND CITY	STATE	HOUSING PLANS
86.	☐☐☐☐☐☐	OR		☐☐	**87.** on campus ○ 1 / off campus ○ 2 / with parent ○ 3
88.	2ND FEDERAL SCHOOL CODE ☐☐☐☐☐☐	OR	NAME OF COLLEGE / ADDRESS AND CITY	☐☐	**89.** on campus ○ 1 / off campus ○ 2 / with parent ○ 3
90.	3RD FEDERAL SCHOOL CODE ☐☐☐☐☐☐	OR	NAME OF COLLEGE / ADDRESS AND CITY	☐☐	**91.** on campus ○ 1 / off campus ○ 2 / with parent ○ 3
92.	4TH FEDERAL SCHOOL CODE ☐☐☐☐☐☐	OR	NAME OF COLLEGE / ADDRESS AND CITY	☐☐	**93.** on campus ○ 1 / off campus ○ 2 / with parent ○ 3
94.	5TH FEDERAL SCHOOL CODE ☐☐☐☐☐☐	OR	NAME OF COLLEGE / ADDRESS AND CITY	☐☐	**95.** on campus ○ 1 / off campus ○ 2 / with parent ○ 3
96.	6TH FEDERAL SCHOOL CODE ☐☐☐☐☐☐	OR	NAME OF COLLEGE / ADDRESS AND CITY	☐☐	**97.** on campus ○ 1 / off campus ○ 2 / with parent ○ 3

Step Seven: Please read, sign, and date.

By signing this application, you agree, if asked, to provide information that will verify the accuracy of your completed form. This information may include your U.S. or state income tax forms. Also, you certify that you (1) will use federal and/or state student financial aid only to pay the cost of attending an institution of higher education, (2) are not in default on a federal student loan or have made satisfactory arrangements to repay it, (3) do not owe money back on a federal student grant or have made satisfactory arrangements to repay it, (4) will notify your school if you default on a federal student loan, and (5) understand that **the Secretary of Education has the authority to verify information reported on this application with the Internal Revenue Service.** If you purposely give false or misleading information, you may be fined $10,000, sent to prison, or both.

98. Date this form was completed.

MONTH ☐☐ / DAY ☐☐ / 2001 ○ or 2002 ○

99. Student signature (Sign in box)

> 1 **FOR INFORMATION ONLY.**

Parent signature (one parent whose information is provided in Step Four) (Sign in box)

> 2 **DO NOT SUBMIT.**

If this form was filled out by someone other than you, your spouse, or your parent(s), that person must complete this part.

Preparer's name, firm, and address

_____
_____
_____

100. Preparer's Social Security Number (or 101)
☐☐☐ – ☐☐ – ☐☐☐☐

101. Employer ID number (or 100)
☐☐ – ☐☐☐☐☐☐☐

102. Preparer's signature and date
1

SCHOOL USE ONLY: Federal School Code

D/O ○ 1   ☐☐☐☐☐☐

FAA SIGNATURE
1

MDE USE ONLY:
Special Handle ☐☐ – ☐☐☐☐☐

Notes for questions 59–83 (page 5) Step Four: Who is considered a parent in this step?

Read these notes to determine who is considered a parent for purposes of this form. **Answer all questions in Step Four about them**, even if you do not live with them.

If your parents are both living and married to each other, answer the questions about them.

If your parent is widowed or single, answer the questions about that parent. If your widowed parent has remarried as of today, answer the questions about that parent **and** the person whom your parent married (your stepparent).

If your parents have divorced or separated, answer the questions about the parent you lived with more during the past 12 months. (If you did not live with one parent more than the other, give answers about the parent who provided more financial support during the last 12 months, or during the most recent year that you actually received support from a parent.) If this parent has remarried as of today, answer the questions on the rest of this form about that parent **and** the person whom your parent married (your stepparent).

Notes for question 64 (page 5)

Include in your parents' household (see notes, above, for who is considered a parent):
- your parents and yourself, even if you don't live with your parents, and
- your parents' other children if (a) your parents will provide more than half of their support from July 1, 2001 through June 30, 2002 or (b) the children could answer "No" to every question in Step Three, and
- other people if they now live with your parents, your parents provide more than half of their support, and your parents will continue to provide more than half of their support from July 1, 2001 through June 30, 2002.

Notes for questions 65 (page 5) and 85 (page 6)

Always count yourself as a college student. **Do not include your parents.** Include others only if they will attend at least half time in 2001-2002 a program that leads to a college degree or certificate.

Notes for question 84 (page 6)

Include in your (and your spouse's) household:
- yourself (and your spouse, if you have one), and
- your children, if you will provide more than half of their support from July 1, 2001 through June 30, 2002, and
- other people if they now live with you, and you provide more than half of their support, and you will continue to provide more than half of their support from July 1, 2001 through June 30, 2002.

Information on the Privacy Act and use of your Social Security Number

We use the information that you provide on this form to determine if you are eligible to receive federal student financial aid and the amount that you are eligible to receive. Section 483 of the Higher Education Act of 1965, as amended, gives us the authority to ask you and your parents these questions, and to collect the Social Security Numbers of you and your parents.

State and institutional student financial aid programs may also use the information that you provide on this form to determine if you are eligible to receive state and institutional aid and the need that you have for such aid. Therefore, we will disclose the information that you provide on this form to each institution you list in questions 86–97, state agencies in your state of legal residence, and the state agencies of the states in which the colleges that you list in questions 86–97 are located.

If you are applying solely for federal aid, you must answer all of the following questions that apply to you: 1–9, 13–15, 24, 27–28, 31–32, 35, 36–40, 42–49, 52–66, 69–74, 76-85, and 98–99. If you do not answer these questions, you will not receive federal aid.

Without your consent, we may disclose information that you provide to entities under a published "routine use." Under such a routine use, we may disclose information to third parties that we have authorized to assist us in administering the above programs; to other federal agencies under computer matching programs, such as those with the Internal Revenue Service, Social Security Administration, Selective Service System, Immigration and Naturalization Service, and Veterans Administration; to your parents or spouse; and to members of Congress if you ask them to help you with student aid questions.

If the federal government, the U.S. Department of Education, or an employee of the U.S. Department of Education is involved in litigation, we may send information to the Department of Justice, or a court or adjudicative body, if the disclosure is related to financial aid and certain conditions are met. In addition, we may send your information to a foreign, federal, state, or local enforcement agency if the information that you submitted indicates a violation or potential violation of law, for which that agency has jurisdiction for investigation or prosecution. Finally, we may send information regarding a claim that is determined to be valid and overdue to a consumer reporting agency. This information includes identifiers from the record; the amount, status, and history of the claim; and the program under which the claim arose.

State Certification

By submitting this application, you are giving your state financial aid agency permission to verify any statement on this form and to obtain income tax information for all persons required to report income on this form.

The Paperwork Reduction Act of 1995

The Paperwork Reduction Act of 1995 says that no one is required to respond to a collection of information unless it displays a valid OMB control number, which for this form is 1845-0001. The time required to complete this form is estimated to be one hour, including time to review instructions, search data resources, gather the data needed, and complete and review the information collection. If you have comments about this estimate or suggestions for improving this form, please write to: U.S. Department of Education, Washington DC 20202-4651.

We may request additional information from you to ensure efficient application processing operations. We will collect this additional information only as needed and on a voluntary basis.

Worksheets

Do not mail these worksheets in with your application.
Keep these worksheets; your school may ask to see them.

Worksheet A

Calendar Year 2000

For question 44 Student/Spouse		For question 78 Parent(s)
$	Earned income credit from IRS Form 1040–line 60a; 1040A–line 38a; 1040EZ–line 8a; or Telefile–line L	$
$	Additional child tax credit from IRS Form 1040–line 62 or 1040A–line 39	$
$	Welfare benefits, including Temporary Assistance for Needy Families (TANF). Don't include food stamps.	$
$	Social Security benefits received that were not taxed (such as SSI)	$
$ ⎯ Enter in question 44.		Enter in question 78. ⎯ $

Worksheet B

Calendar Year 2000

For question 45 Student/Spouse		For question 79 Parent(s)
$	Payments to tax-deferred pension and savings plans (paid directly or withheld from earnings), including amounts reported on the W-2 Form in Box 13, codes D, E, F, G, H, and S	$
$	IRA deductions and payments to self-employed SEP, SIMPLE, and Keogh and other qualified plans from IRS Form 1040–total of lines 23 + 29 or 1040A–line 16	$
$	Child support **received** for all children. Don't include foster care or adoption payments.	$
$	Tax exempt interest income from IRS Form 1040–line 8b or 1040A–line 8b	$
$	Foreign income exclusion from IRS Form 2555–line 43 or 2555EZ–line 18	$
$	Untaxed portions of pensions from IRS Form 1040–lines (15a minus 15b) + (16a minus 16b) or 1040A–lines (11a minus 11b) + (12a minus 12b) excluding rollovers	$
$	Credit for federal tax on special fuels from IRS Form 4136–line 9 – nonfarmers only	$
$	Housing, food, and other living allowances paid to members of the military, clergy, and others (including cash payments and cash value of benefits)	$
$	Veterans noneducation benefits such as Disability, Death Pension, or Dependency & Indemnity Compensation (DIC) and/or VA Educational Work-Study allowances	$
$	Any other untaxed income or benefits not reported elsewhere on Worksheets A and B, such as worker's compensation, untaxed portions of railroad retirement benefits, Black Lung Benefits, Refugee Assistance, etc. **Don't include** student aid, Workforce Investment Act educational benefits, or benefits from flexible spending arrangements, e.g., cafeteria plans.	$
$	Cash **received**, or any money paid on your behalf, not reported elsewhere on this form	XXXXXXXX
$ ⎯ Enter in question 45.		Enter in question 79. ⎯ $

Worksheet C

Calendar Year 2000

For question 46 Student/Spouse		For question 80 Parent(s)
$	Education credits (Hope and Lifetime Learning tax credits) from IRS Form 1040-line 46 or 1040A-line 29	$
$	Child support **paid** because of divorce or separation. Do not include support for children in your (or your parents') household, as reported in question 84 (or question 64 for your parents).	$
$	Taxable earnings from Federal Work-Study or other need-based work programs	$
$	Student grant, scholarship, and fellowship aid, including AmeriCorps awards, that was reported to the IRS in your (or your parents') adjusted gross income	$
$ ⎯ Enter in question 46.		Enter in question 80. ⎯ $